# DESIGN THINKING FOR ENTREPRENEURS AND SMALL BUSINESSES

## PUTTING THE POWER OF DESIGN TO WORK

*Beverly Rudkin Ingle*

**Apress®**

*Design Thinking for Entrepreneurs and Small Businesses: Putting the Power of Design to Work*

ISBN-13 (pbk): 978-1-4302-6181-0

ISBN-13 (electronic): 978-1-4302-6182-7

Trademarked names, logos, and images may appear in this book. Rather than use a trademark symbol with every occurrence of a trademarked name, logo, or image we use the names, logos, and images only in an editorial fashion and to the benefit of the trademark owner, with no intention of infringement of the trademark.

The use in this publication of trade names, trademarks, service marks, and similar terms, even if they are not identified as such, is not to be taken as an expression of opinion as to whether or not they are subject to proprietary rights.

While the advice and information in this book are believed to be true and accurate at the date of publication, neither the authors nor the editors nor the publisher can accept any legal responsibility for any errors or omissions that may be made. The publisher makes no warranty, express or implied, with respect to the material contained herein.

President and Publisher: Paul Manning
Acquisitions Editor: Jeff Olson
Editorial Board: Steve Anglin, Mark Beckner, Ewan Buckingham, Gary Cornell,
    Louise Corrigan, James DeWolf, Jonathan Gennick, Jonathan Hassell,
    Robert Hutchinson, Michelle Lowman, James Markham, Matthew Moodie,
    Jeff Olson, Jeffrey Pepper, Douglas Pundick, Ben Renow-Clarke,
    Dominic Shakeshaft, Gwenan Spearing, Matt Wade, Steve Weiss, Tom Welsh
Coordinating Editor: Rita Fernando
Copy Editor: Laura Poole
Compositor: SPi Global
Indexer: SPi Global
Cover Designer: Anna Ishchenko

Distributed to the book trade worldwide by Springer Science+Business Media New York, 233 Spring Street, 6th Floor, New York, NY 10013. Phone 1-800-SPRINGER, fax (201) 348-4505, e-mail orders-ny@springer-sbm.com, or visit www.springeronline.com. Apress Media, LLC is a California LLC and the sole member (owner) is Springer Science + Business Media Finance Inc (SSBM Finance Inc). SSBM Finance Inc is a Delaware corporation.

For information on translations, please e-mail rights@apress.com, or visit www.apress.com.

Apress and friends of ED books may be purchased in bulk for academic, corporate, or promotional use. eBook versions and licenses are also available for most titles. For more information, reference our Special Bulk Sales–eBook Licensing web page at www.apress.com/bulk-sales.

Any source code or other supplementary materials referenced by the author in this text is available to readers at www.apress.com. For detailed information about how to locate your book's source code, go to www.apress.com/source-code/.

## Apress Business: The Unbiased Source of Business Information

Apress business books provide essential information and practical advice, each written for practitioners by recognized experts. Busy managers and professionals in all areas of the business world—and at all levels of technical sophistication—look to our books for the actionable ideas and tools they need to solve problems, update and enhance their professional skills, make their work lives easier, and capitalize on opportunity.

Whatever the topic on the business spectrum—entrepreneurship, finance, sales, marketing, management, regulation, information technology, among others—Apress has been praised for providing the objective information and unbiased advice you need to excel in your daily work life. Our authors have no axes to grind; they understand they have one job only—to deliver up-to-date, accurate information simply, concisely, and with deep insight that addresses the real needs of our readers.

It is increasingly hard to find information—whether in the news media, on the Internet, and now all too often in books—that is even-handed and has your best interests at heart. We therefore hope that you enjoy this book, which has been carefully crafted to meet our standards of quality and unbiased coverage.

We are always interested in your feedback or ideas for new titles. Perhaps you'd even like to write a book yourself. Whatever the case, reach out to us at editorial@apress.com and an editor will respond swiftly. Incidentally, at the back of this book, you will find a list of useful related titles. Please visit us at www.apress.com to sign up for newsletters and discounts on future purchases.

*The Apress Business Team*

*In memory of my mama.*

# Contents

Foreword . . . . . . . . . . . . . . . . . . . . . . . . . . . . . . . . . . . . . . . . . . . . . ix

About the Author. . . . . . . . . . . . . . . . . . . . . . . . . . . . . . . . . . . . . . . xi

Acknowledgments . . . . . . . . . . . . . . . . . . . . . . . . . . . . . . . . . . . . . xiii

Preface. . . . . . . . . . . . . . . . . . . . . . . . . . . . . . . . . . . . . . . . . . . . . . . xv

Chapter 1:    Introduction to Design Thinking · · · · · · · · · · · · · · · · · · · · ·1

Chapter 2:    The Role of Research in Design Thinking · · · · · · · · · · · ·17

Chapter 3:    Designing a Business Strategy · · · · · · · · · · · · · · · · · · · ·31

Chapter 4:    Designing Live Customer Experiences · · · · · · · · · · · · ·39

Chapter 5:    Designing Digital Customer Experiences · · · · · · · · · · · ·53

Chapter 6:    Designing Services and Service Delivery· · · · · · · · · · ·67

Chapter 7:    Designing Marketing · · · · · · · · · · · · · · · · · · · · · · · · · ·77

Chapter 8:    Designing for Change · · · · · · · · · · · · · · · · · · · · · · · · · ·93

Chapter 9:    Designing for Growth · · · · · · · · · · · · · · · · · · · · · · · · · ·103

Appendix A: Case Studies· · · · · · · · · · · · · · · · · · · · · · · · · · · · · · · ·117

Appendix B: Metrics for Design Thinking · · · · · · · · · · · · · · · · · · · ·127

Appendix C: Glossary of Design Thinking Jargon · · · · · · · · · · · · · ·133

Appendix D: Resources · · · · · · · · · · · · · · · · · · · · · · · · · · · · · · · · · ·137

Index . . . . . . . . . . . . . . . . . . . . . . . . . . . . . . . . . . . . . . . . . . . . . . . . .149

# Foreword

While I was having dinner with Steve Myers of CERN, he shared with me some of his stories of the development and first operation of the Large Hadron Collider and his frustrations with the media who by and large sought to scare the general public with stories of tiny black holes that could endanger the entire planet. His team of physicists was largely unprepared for the media assault and fared badly, which unfortunately led to many apocalyptic stories in the European tabloids. Listening sympathetically to this story, I remembered something my father once told me, "You can't be good at everything. Concentrate on what you know you're good at, make good guesses at the things that are within reach of your understanding, and for everything else take the best counsel you can find." It's advice I carry around with me like an old heirloom watch, and it's advice Steve and his team could have used. He's an expert physicist, but no expert at media relations.

Technology drives democratization, from areas as diverse as the political arena (think of Twitter's role in the Arab Spring) to the arts (Adobe Premiere, the leading filmmakers' tool, runs quite happily on my old MacBook Pro) and of course, the Internet start-up culture that has opened up resources—previously only available to large enterprises—to the bedroom entrepreneur through cloud computing. There's no end in sight. In the next few years, manufacturing capabilities will move from the fabrication plant to the garage by way of affordable 3D printing technology. It's a rosy story; finally we have at our disposal all the technology and services required to harness our creative impulses. We can move from a sketch on the back of a taxi receipt to a highly successful product or service used by millions in a matter of months.

But how do we leverage these technologies and services to our best advantage if we don't also have access to resources that help us build our strategic vision and entrepreneurial dexterity? I want to introduce you to someone who gives you that access.

I first met Beverly Rudkin Ingle in the Hilton bar at South by Southwest 2012. I was a little grumpy and a little tired, having traveled for sixteen hours from London, expecting a few days of relentless Texan sunshine only to be met with weather not that different than a typical English summer day—wind and driving rain. I was inspired, though, after listening to Dave Morin evangelize on the importance of driving the emotional context of his business, Path. As I nursed a gin and tonic and thought about what the days ahead might hold, I gradually began to be sucked into the conversation this astute, sassy Texan woman next to me was having with the founders of a now highly successful digital agency. As she wove her stories, I began to focus less on the college basketball playing on the bank of TVs behind the bar and more on her persuasive narrative. Beverly is many things to many people, and to me she is nothing less than a brilliant storyteller.

Soon I found myself deep into an elaboration of her theory—no that's wrong, her mission—to democratize the often opaque process of business/product innovation and evolution. Beverly's key message is that big companies don't rely on luck. They leverage the power of design thinking. So why can't entrepreneurs and small business owners do the same if they are equipped with a few easy-to-use, commonsense tools?

Now thanks to her book, they can. The good news: it's much easier than physics.

*—Paul Ramshaw, Principal Product Manager,*
*hybris software: an SAP company, Munich, Germany.*

# About the Author

**Beverly Rudkin Ingle** founded Resilient by Design, a marketing strategy and innovation management consultancy based in San Antonio, Texas, where she works with clients from a variety of industries to understand and leverage the design process to create stronger, more profitable businesses. Equally left-brained and right-brained, she is a strategist through and through, and she is passionate about developing strong brands that resonate with local consumers as a means to helping entrepreneurs and local economies succeed.

A Fellow among the inaugural cohort of the Leading by Design Fellows Program of the California College of the Arts, Beverly has used the skills she's learned to help companies grow, weather change, and become more profitable anchors in their local communities.

# Acknowledgments

I am thrilled to have this opportunity to extend my sincere gratitude to the following people for their inspiration, guidance, and support in creating this book.

My husband and best friend, Joe, for his unwavering love and belief in my ability to pull this off, and his tolerance of baseball caps.

My daughters, Anna, Katie, Evelyn, and Victoria, who were wonderfully patient and understanding and who learned that if I was typing on the computer with earbuds plugged in, I was working and shouldn't be interrupted unless there was blood, broken bones, or barf.

My daddy, Jack; my mama, Bobbi; my dad, Jerry; and my in-laws, J. and Kathy; for the truly special love, encouragement, and support that you can get only from parents, present and in spirit.

My foil and partner-in-crime, Paul R., who made me stop and pay attention—and gave me a push—at South by Southwest.

My faithful friends and cheerleaders—Angel, Chris, Jeanette, Jeremy, Mary Katherine, Melissa, Michele, Missy, Paul S., Sandy, and Susan M.—whose enthusiasm buoys me when I need it most.

My colleague and friend Susan Worthman, director of the Leading by Design Fellows Program at the California College of the Arts, who embraced the tornado and encouraged my enthusiasm for change.

My editor, Jeff Olson; coordinating editor Rita Fernando; and Apress Media for the invaluable guidance, confidence and opportunity.

And my tenth-grade English teacher, Tom Vannatta, who has no idea how much of an influence he was.

# Preface

The entrepreneurial spirit in the United States is dynamic, determined, and laced with fantastic tales of self-made millionaires and enviable success stories. There's a great deal of mystique surrounding those tales, which I attribute to our country's unique reputation of being the land of opportunity. Entrepreneurs have created more than 27 million small businesses according to 2010 data.[1] If you are holding this book, you probably are one of them, and you're looking for your next competitive advantage.

When I first heard the phrase "design thinking," I had been on a quest for the next competitive advantage for my clients and myself. Instinctively, I knew the next step had to be big and bold; it had to embrace change and be purposeful in its approach to business challenges. It also had to make the consumer or customer a priority like never before. I wasn't sure where to turn, but a series of fortuitous conversations and research on the Internet led me to design thinking.

The methodology was what I had been searching for, and by all accounts, it was successful. Large corporations have been leveraging design thinking for years, albeit using various other terminologies. Procter & Gamble, Apple, British Airways, Roche, Samsung, and other corporations of their magnitude put design thinking principles to work for their collective success every day.

"If the big boys are doing it," I thought, "then there must be measurable value."

I discovered that there was—and continues to be—measurable value, and quite a lot of it. I also discovered that design thinking was still sequestered in corporate boardrooms. Access was limited to those with big ideas and deep pockets, available through major agencies and consultancies and often with hefty price tags.

For those of us not leading large corporations but those 27 million small businesses, access to design thinking was nearly nonexistent. I wrote this book to change that. A shift to purposeful, customer-centric business practices that would be sustainable over the long run starts with the small businesses that create the backbone of our economy. That shift starts now.

---

[1] See http://www.sba.gov/sites/default/files/FAQ_Sept_2012.pdf.

Without consulting fees, project retainers, contract commitments, or even a boardroom, you now have access to some of the most productive design thinking principles, methodologies, and activities that you can put to work immediately. All you need is enthusiasm, an open mind, some markers, a white board or flip chart, a few stacks of sticky notes, and this book, and you're ready to go.

At a glance, *Design Thinking for Entrepreneurs and Small Businesses* guides you through the following:

> Chapter 1—A detailed but digestible introduction to design thinking
>
> Chapter 2—The importance of research, why you cannot skimp on it, and why you don't have to
>
> Chapter 3—Designing a business strategy, and why it isn't an oxymoron
>
> Chapter 4—Designing live customer experiences and why first impressions will always be meaningful
>
> Chapter 5—Designing digital customer experiences and how to create connections with customers
>
> Chapter 6—Designing services and service delivery and how efficiency benefits your business and your customers
>
> Chapter 7—Designing marketing and branding and why it is—and should be—so much more than your logo
>
> Chapter 8—Designing for change in your business model, market, or competitive environment
>
> Chapter 9—Designing for growth and why growth does not stop

I included four appendixes filled with additional data, templates, and case studies to help guide you along your discovery and implementation of design thinking.

Design thinking has yet to reach its peak of influence, because until now it wasn't readily available to entrepreneurs and small businesses. You, dear reader, are at the vanguard of the next competitive advantage: design thinking. Congratulations for taking this first step. Now, go show the big boys what you're made of.

# Introduction to Design Thinking

## Combining Creativity and Analysis in Business

In the past couple of years, the term *design* has been thrown around quite a bit in various business contexts. We've heard of user design, experience design, social design, integrated design, service design, and place-based design, in addition to the term with which we are most familiar: graphic design.

Although design was once the sole domain of graphic designers—those professionals with the artistic skill to create logos, advertisements, signage, and printed materials of all sorts—you can now find a plethora of professionals in other industries describing themselves as designers. Depending on how they approach their work, the term *designer* might be quite applicable, and here is why:

> Design in its current use in business vernacular describes a data-driven, purposeful intent behind an action, and that intent occurs to affect a specific, measurable business outcome.

If you approach your business with this kind of intent, regardless of its industry, size, age, niche within the marketplace, or geographic location (or lack thereof for online-only enterprises), then you, too, are a designer.

If you can begin to think like a designer and learn some of the tools designers use regularly to drive growth and success, then myriad doors of possibility will open.

---

■ **Note**   No matter what kind of business you're in, and no matter the size, it will be of benefit when you and your fellow employees consider yourself designers. It's a useful—and profitable— way to plan and execute your initiatives.

---

# What Is Design Thinking?

Do an Internet search of "design thinking" through your favorite search tool, and you'll turn up an absurd number of results (several hundred thousand at the time of this writing). In the simplest of terms, design thinking is an exploratory approach to problem solving that includes and balances both analytical and creative thought processes.

Tim Brown, CEO of IDEO, a renowned design and innovation firm, and arguably the first champion of design thinking in business, wrote this of design thinking in *Change By Design:* "Insofar as it is open-ended, open-minded and iterative, a process fed by design thinking will feel chaotic to those experiencing it for the first time."[1]

No truer words have been written about design thinking. It will feel chaotic the first time, and probably the second and third times, and maybe even the fourth time you put it to use. Design thinking is not a typical skill set learned in business school, but a valuable skill that should be embraced by all business professionals, not just those in a "creative" industry or for whom design is front-and-center in their job description. Design thinking is an egalitarian skill set that can be learned, practiced, and championed by professionals across industries and job titles.

Design thinking is largely nonlinear and fluid, as most explorations are—or at least should be. A true exploration is not a forced march between Point A and Point B, but a meandering trail that ends at the defined destination of Point B yet allows for the flexibility to observe the landscape along the way and, perhaps, discover something new or previously overlooked. The circuitous nature of design thinking does not derive from a designer's lack of the discipline needed to be organized and deliberate. Much to the contrary, design thinking is purposefully intended to be circuitous and fluid as a challenge to the conventional means of problem solving.

---

[1] Tim Brown, *Change By Design* (New York: HarperCollins, 2009), p. 17.

We are experienced in (and some may argue trained ir next?" when working toward solving a problem. (I blar necessarily rigid adherence to a sequential order in pr _ design thinking, there isn't always a specific "next" to which we _ proceed. Each phase of design thinking could yield multiple "nexts" as possibilities, and it is up to us—the design thinking team—to determine which "next" to pursue. Admittedly, this can be a little confusing at first.

Perhaps most important, design thinking is an iterative and rapid process that can be applied to even the most confounding business challenges, and it is a strategic activity that will identify clear opportunities that you can act on quickly.

# The Phases of Design Thinking

Given design thinking's adaptable, flowing nature, no one can truly say with strong conviction, "This is the way design thinking happens." There are defined phases in the approach that serve as excellent signposts indicating you are making progress. However, the work that happens within each phase can vary wildly depending on the challenge at hand.

Let's begin with a high-level review of the phases of design thinking, after which we'll dive deeper into each to better understand what happens and how it fits into the bigger design-thinking picture.

## Phase I: Understand

Understanding your business challenge is imperative to identifying and creating a solution, and the degree of understanding goes well beyond that of conjecture or your previous history with challenges of a similar nature.

## Phase II: Define

Once you understand the challenge at a level of detail that reveals subtle nuances you likely would have missed without taking the time to develop that understanding, you can clearly define in specific terms what the challenge is and why it needs to be addressed.

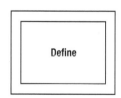

## Phase III: Ideate

Now that the challenge is defined and you know what problem needs to be solved, you can unleash your creativity and begin imagining solutions. Ideation is by far the phase that everyone enjoys most, and because of that, many teams get bogged down here. Teams are also tempted to jump ahead to this phase, completely forgoing Understand and Define. Avoid both tendencies at all costs, or you very likely will generate a wealth of fantastic ideas that aren't relevant to the challenge or go off on fantastic tangents.

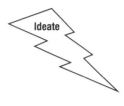

## Phase IV: Prototype

Once you draw the ideation phase to a close, the next step is to cull through the idea inventory and select the cream of the crop. These are the ideas you'll take into the prototype phase. Be judicious in your selection of ideas—specifically the quantity of them—because you will need to create a prototype of each one. As a good rule of thumb, you'll want to plan on prototyping at least two or three ideas. Prototyping will start to give your ideas depth, so you can get an impression of how they will take form in reality. Prototypes aren't always tangible items. It is just as important to prototype a service, experience, process, or other intangible.

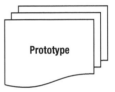

---

**Note**   In design thinking, you prototype not just products but also services, experiences, processes, and other things most would consider intangible.

---

## Phase V: Test

Testing will help you save money during development and avoid potential disaster. This sounds dramatic, but it's true. Testing will keep you from committing resources to a project only to find out that you were on the wrong path. The upside is that testing doesn't have to be complicated or expensive.

There you have it: design thinking, a process of only fi'
is critically important to understand about design
the process does not always consist of a direct line  ̣ ̣
Point B through the phases. As you work through the proce>>,  ,
may find you need to back up and repeat a phase. For example, you
could find that in the Define phase, you don't have quite enough data
to help you clearly articulate the challenge you're facing, and therefore you need to go back to the Understand phase and do a bit more
research. Or you could discover in the Prototype phase that one
(or more) of your ideas can't be constructed as you had hoped, and you
need to Ideate some more. You could even discover in the Test phase
that your prototypes all bombed, and you need to start over with the
Understand phase.

How you move through the design-thinking process is determined largely
by the quality of your work in each phase. Stay focused on each phase as
you're in it, without taking a look at the horizon for the next one. If you
look too far ahead, you might miss something critical.

# A Deeper Dive

Now that you've waded into the water and have a better understanding of
design thinking, it is time to take off the floaties and dive in to get a more
in-depth grasp of each phase of the process.

## Understand

Creating a solution to your business challenge is next to impossible without some clear understanding of what your challenge entails. The nature
of the challenge may appear to be one thing on the surface and something
else entirely once you peel back the visible layers. Consider this example:
a local hospital has seen its share of births decline since a competing facility opened nearby. The new facility offers a few distinct patient benefits,
such as advanced security and a catered dinner in-room for the new parents, which the local hospital doesn't offer. The local hospital leadership
believes those benefits at the competing facility are luring patients away
from their hospital.

On the surface, that scenario seems plausible, and the local hospital leadership makes plans to counter the competitor's benefits with some new
ones of their own, such as an easier admission process and limo service
for parents to take their babies home. A competitive environment with
more options and benefits for the patient seems like a smart business
move, right?

How does the local hospital leadership know that their new benefits will sway a patient's choice? Have they talked to their prospective patient group? Have they asked expectant parents what services and benefits they want from a hospital, and which are most important to them? Have they asked new parents why they chose the hospital where their child was born?

Rather than rushing to judgment and adding benefits as the answer, the local hospital leadership needs to take the time to understand their potential patients' needs and wants. How can middle-aged men understand what the twenty- and thirty-something expectant moms need and want in a hospital? The best way to do that is through research, which I cover more extensively in Chapter 2.

More often than not, especially when revenue is on the line and a business's key performance indicators are watched very closely by investors and other stakeholders, leadership will make a decision based on their past experience in the industry, a measured guess based on market trends, their gut instinct, or a combination of all three, when what is needed most is accurate data derived from research. Although taking the time to do the research during the Understand phase cannot guarantee a better performance than going with your gut, it will give you a much stronger and more accurate foundation from which to make decisions and will give you more confidence that the decisions you make are the best options.

# Define

At the conclusion of the Understand phase, you should have a fair amount of data, both quantitative (think numbers, scaled responses, answers that can be measured) and qualitative (typically responses to open-ended questions). The quantity of data is completely dependent on the extent of your research and the nature of your industry. At a minimum, you need enough data for developing a comprehensive assessment of the situation or challenge at hand.

From that assessment, you can define the specific business challenge you face. Continuing our example of the local hospital, let's say the assessment of the research data reveals that the patients going to the competitor facility aren't choosing to give birth there because of its benefits but because it offers a more advanced level of neonatal care, which calms expectant moms' fears of possible health complications for the baby during birth.

That's the "a ha!" moment for the local hospital leadership.

The opportunity to change patient behavior and regain market share lies not in creating additional benefits for new parents. The opportunity lies in making appropriate investments in talent and technology to develop a neonatal unit. The business challenge defined becomes: "Design an advanced-care neonatal unit for the local hospital and allocate the funds needed to develop the unit to be competitive in the market." That's quite a bit different from how the business challenge for the local hospital might have been defined if the Understand phase was bypassed.

# Ideate

As mentioned earlier, this is the phase that people enjoy most. With the challenge defined, now is the time to dream up how to solve it. Brainstorming, another name for ideating, dominates this phase of design thinking. To get the most out of brainstorming, you truly need to suspend reality, disregard the typical parameters for business operations, check your ego at the door, and repeat to yourself, "There are no bad ideas."

Be very deliberate in identifying the individuals you want to be on your brainstorming team. The nature of your business challenge will help dictate who those people are. Your goal here is a heterogeneous group built around a core of individuals that closely resembles your target market through demographics and psychographics. Diversity is your friend. Don't default to including only your senior leadership or subject matter experts during the Ideate phase. Branch out and include a mix of employees from various levels in the organization, including someone from operations, who will lend a broad perspective. You may consider inviting trusted vendors, thought partners, and even friends and family members to join you to offer an outsider's viewpoint, as well. Entrepreneurs might consider including funding partners.

Although diversity in your brainstorming group is important, the number of people involved is equally important. You need enough to create some enthusiasm and provide varying viewpoints, but not so many that the activities get unwieldy or warring factions of opinions arise. I prefer groups of no fewer than three and no more than ten.

Once you have your brainstorming team selected, schedule a two-hour block of time in which to brainstorm. You'll need at least one two-hour block and perhaps additional blocks depending on the nature of the challenge to be solved and the productivity of the group. Remember, you will need to prototype at least two solid ideas for testing, so don't get caught up on one great idea and decide you're done. Keep exploring the challenge from all angles.

▓ **Tip**   While there are no bad ideas during the Ideate phase, they can sometimes be off topic. Honor those off-topic ideas by documenting them in a "parking lot" area to hold for future consideration.

Brainstorming or ideation sessions can easily go off the rails and disintegrate into wasted time and occasionally hurt feelings. Here are five key rules to keep your group on track, productive, and positive.

1. **Declare your intention**: Under no circumstances should you enter a brainstorming session without a clearly articulated intent of what you aim to get out of it, and be sure to communicate that to your group ahead of time. You want everyone participating to be working toward the same goal in a brainstorming session. By communicating your intent ahead of time, you prime the pump, so to speak, and your team will likely spend some time thinking about your challenge in advance of the session.

2. **Everyone is equal**: In the real world—the one outside of the brainstorming session—the president of the company carries more weight than an accounting assistant. During brainstorming, everyone is equal regardless of his or her role in the company or place in the hierarchy. There is no seniority, and the only authority in the room is the one chosen to be the moderator. Everyone is free to speak, and everyone is obliged to listen to the speaker. Period.

3. **All things in moderation**: Prior to the session, select someone to be the moderator. This person should be adept at facilitating conversations, asking pertinent questions, and documenting what is said or done. This person must also be comfortable redirecting the conversation if it's gone off on a tangent, appropriately interrupting if someone is dominating the conversation, and moving the discussion along if it gets bogged down in one particular area. Ideally, the moderator you choose has no "skin in the game" and therefore no self-interest in the outcome of the brainstorming. If you can afford to contract with an independent moderator or facilitator, do so, particularly if you have a headstrong group that needs to be guided by a firm and unbiased hand.

4. **Write it down**: Every idea, thought, or question needs to be documented. Do not rely on anyone's memory to recall the outcomes from your brainstorming session. Documentation is key! You'll want to be able to refer to what occurred with accuracy. I prefer to document brainstorming sessions in two ways: by themselves or combined. The first method is with sticky notes. Choose three colors: one for ideas, one for thoughts, and one for questions. Each idea, thought, or question gets written on its own color-coded note. I repeat, *each* gets its own note. You may want to sort these later, and if you have to cut a sticky-note in half because it contained two separate ideas, it's likely the halves will get lost. The second method is to document the discussion on a white board, but again assign a different color to each statement category (idea, thought, question). Be sure you photograph the white board before erasing it. Every cell phone has a camera; use it. In fact, have several people take several pictures as a precaution.

5. **Let the sillies out**: Whether your group is experienced brainstormers or new to the activity, they will inevitably feel a bit awkward at the beginning, and that usually leads to a case of the sillies: outlandish ideas that contextually make no sense but are contributed as a kind of joke to break the ice. That's normal and okay. Just let the sillies flow and get them out of the group's system so they can concentrate on the challenge at hand. Two things to note: the sillies should not be confused with "bad ideas" because there are no bad ideas during brainstorming. Second, if you have a recurrence of the sillies toward the end of the brainstorming session, you've run too long and it's time to wrap up, even if there is still time left on the clock.

Tying back into our neonatal unit example, your group may have ideas ranging anywhere from developing its own unit to collaborating with another provider to supplementing its own services to tapping into emerging technology to fill the gap.

# Prototype

At the end of brainstorming, you likely have a slew of ideas occupying space along the continuum from "awesome" to "what the hell were we thinking?" You may be a bit overwhelmed with the volume of ideas and struggling to sift the chaff from the most delightful morsels. This is where the Prototype phase begins, and you start to see its value.

Once you're finished with the Ideate phase and have moved into the Prototype phase, it's time to put the business operations parameters back into play and view your ideas through the lens of reality. In doing so, you can begin to separate your brainstorming ideas into categories of what is doable, what is possible, and what is so far-reaching that it will require too many resources to pull off.

---

■ **Tip** After you've sorted the ideas from the Ideation phase, pack up the notes about the far-reaching ones and save them. You never know when they might trigger other ideas down the road or evolve into possibilities.

---

Now that you've organized your ideas, meet with your operations team or leader and take a close look at which ideas are the most viable to try given your current state of resources—capital, time, and talent—and which could make the greatest positive impact toward solving your business challenge. Where these factors overlap is where the opportunity lies.

Visually, this looks like a Venn diagram (Figure 1-1).

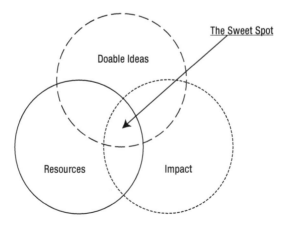

**Figure 1-1.** Where your available resources, doable ideas, and potential impact overlap is the "sweet spot," the area in which your opportunities lie.

The ideas that lie in the sweet spot should be the ones for which prototypes are developed. Wondering what you should do if there aren't any ideas in the sweet spot? Go back to the Ideate phase and brainstorm some more.

Ideally, you will have two or three ideas in the sweet spot. Trying to prototype any more than that will get to be overwhelming and potentially costly. To start building your prototypes, select the idea that you think will require the least amount of resources to be a starting point. It will ease you into the prototype process and is more likely to be a successful and enjoyable activity for your team.

Remember, it doesn't matter if the idea you are prototyping is a material object, a process, or an experience. It still needs to be fleshed out to a point that it can undergo enough viable testing to prove that it works and has the potential to succeed.

Returning to the earlier example of the local hospital that needs to design a neonatal care unit to better compete in its market, the Prototype phase could include a physical mock-up of an actual department, with furniture and equipment, in a repurposed existing space within the hospital. There may be a prototype of new construction needed to create the neonatal care unit. Or perhaps there is a technology solution, such as remote patient monitoring and high-risk protocols, that can be introduced through new workflows and collaborations that need to be prototyped.

Give the prototypes as much detail and specificity as possible. When you enter the Test phase, you'll want to have as complete a prototype as possible so that your test subjects aren't put in the position of providing feedback based on conjecture.

## Test

Now that you have at least two prototypes developed, it's time for the Test phase. Frankly, my blood pressure goes up any time I hear the word *test*, but that's an illogical response with this type of test. Testing prototypes keeps you from charging down the wrong path, and spending way too much money and other resources on a potential solution only to discover that it doesn't work like it should. Testing is a good thing.

Testing can be easy and inexpensive, which is also a good thing. How to test your prototype depends on what it is. We'll cover this in more specificity in the chapters ahead, but we touch on the common elements of testing here.

Your testing participants should mirror the users for whom the solution will remedy the business challenge, and should include key stakeholder groups who are affected by the implementation of the solution. In the local hospital example, the testing participants could include expectant mothers, obstetricians, neonatologists, nurses, respiratory therapists, and facility operations staff—perhaps even mothers of children born in neonatal care units in other hospitals. Gathering feedback from different users and stakeholders will yield an array of perspectives.

Testing is one area in which diversity needs to be controlled. Although you may be testing your ideas among various groups, you will want to organize your testing participants by type—nurses with nurses, and so on—to get the most out of the activity. By keeping like participants together, you can capitalize on their shared knowledge and perspective, which will help keep the testing time shorter and the feedback focused. This will improve the likelihood that they will suggest modifications to the idea.

---

**Tip**   Make sure your testing participants are the types of customers who would use your product or service. If your service is designed for nurses, don't test the service on teachers.

---

How do you find testing participants? Start in your own back yard with your contact list and just ask. You'll be surprised by their willingness to help. However, you may need participants with very specific demographics, like a nurse with more than five years of experience working in a hospital environment. In that case, you can still recruit through your own network by asking your contacts to forward your need on to others they may know. You can also recruit through Craigslist, use Facebook advertising (which is very affordable), or network through professional associations. If there isn't a conflict of interest, you could approach another business entity—such as a hospital system for our nurse example—and uncover opportunities to communicate with and recruit their employees.

Regardless of who your participants are or what you test, the participants need to sign a nondisclosure agreement and a noncompete agreement prior to any discussions of or interactions with your product, service, or process. They also should be made aware that the testing sessions probably will be documented with audio and video recording for research purposes only. If a participant refuses to sign the agreements or does not want to be recorded, I strongly recommend they be excused from the Test phase. When the agreements are signed and complete, you need to give the participants an appropriate overview of the context prior to any testing. Using the local hospital example, it would be critical to explain to the participants the challenge the administration is trying to solve and the solution the prototype represents. Then the participants will be prepared to provide meaningful feedback.

Although testing can be done inexpensively, do not skimp on providing food and beverages. This is not only hospitable and appropriate but also a strategic maneuver to encourage the group to relax and feel welcome. You may also consider offering modest cash compensation. Although not required, it is a smart consideration if the product, service, or process you are testing is complicated, requires a great deal of input or effort on the participant's part, or if recruiting participants becomes difficult.

Keep the testing atmosphere light and relaxed. You want your participants to feel welcomed, comfortable, and valued, and you want to portray yourself and your team as welcoming, open-minded, and collaborative. The location of testing is again dependent on what you are testing. We are all familiar with the stereotypical focus group room with one-way glass, on the other side of which sits the client and his or her entourage observing the testing. Those facilities can be found—and rented—in most large cities. However, that kind of formality and expense is far from necessary. More common locations are on the business's premises, in an online environment, and in the field, particularly if your means of testing does not include focus groups.

As was important during the Ideate phase, documentation is critical in the Test phase. You will want to refer back to what was shared by the participants with accuracy, because their feedback will affect directly the future development of your product, service, or process. During the Test phase, I highly recommend the use of an impartial moderator or facilitator, as well as both written documentation of the testing process and outcomes, and audio/video documentation. As a general rule, once I start recording a testing session, I remind participants that the session is being recorded for documentation only to assist with reporting on the testing outcomes.

Selecting one prototype from our neonatal unit example, new construction of a unit, one testing scenario might consist of participants playing their specific roles—expectant mom, nurse, administrative assistant, physician—as they "walk through" the construction mock-up and narrate their experience. Expectant moms would give input on what they like and what they don't like about the check-in process, what they think is missing in the labor and delivery room that would improve the experience, and what amenities you may have included that don't make an impact. Physicians and nurses would provide feedback on their experiences as well, but because their points of view are entirely different, you'll get different data.

With testing, you are aiming to uncover insights from all users that would culminate in creating a neonatal care unit that satisfies their needs and wants, while at the same time providing a solution to your business challenge, with the specific purpose of shifting market share your way.

Once your stakeholder groups have tested the product, service, or process, gather all of your documentation, give your left brain a jolt, and get ready to analyze the results. It's not as hard as it sounds, really. This kind of analysis involves a lot of compare-and-contrast activity. First, review the data from each stakeholder group on its own merit. Look for common themes in participants' comments, reactions, and suggestions. If you included audio/video documentation, look for common themes in participants' facial expressions and other nonverbal cues, particularly in response to a moderator's questions or as correlated with a specific action as part of the test.

Then look across the stakeholder groups, comparing the common themes you documented during individual group analysis. Themes that are shared across user groups indicate a more universal concern with the product, service, or process, and you'll need to pay close attention to those, because they will affect your work on a larger scale. Themes unique to a stakeholder group may indicate a specific need that should be addressed, but not necessarily with the product, service, or process you are currently testing.

You will follow the same analysis for each of the prototypes you tested. (Are you getting a better understanding of why I recommend limiting your prototypes to only two or three?) Once the analysis is complete for each prototype, you want to pull back and look at the whole picture by comparing the prototypes to one another. Common themes will indicate areas that need to be remedied regardless of which prototype moves forward to production, so acknowledge those but don't spend too much time on them at this point.

Look for the themes unique to a specific prototype and consider their importance to developing a successful solution to your challenge. If one theme is perceived to be more critical than others—perhaps because your most important stakeholder group identified the theme—compare its needs to your available resources. Can you allocate resources appropriately to satisfy the theme's needs and therefore improve the chances of success for the product, service, or process? Conversely, are there several themes that will require smaller investments but collectively yield a bigger effect and potential for success?

By the end of the Test phase, there is a lot of data, some lingering questions, and a bit of gut instinct. However, there are no right answers. The only "right" answers are those derived from that data and those that you determine to be the best for accomplishing your business's goals. Gather your team and review the testing results. Did they prove or disprove the basic premise that one (or more) of the solutions you presented for testing actually will solve the business challenge you face? Did one solution perform better than others, or did they all test well? Did they all fall far below expectations?

If none of the solutions tested performed well, you need to stop and take a hard look to determine why. Answering the "why" will help you determine to what point in the design-thinking process you need to return. Some questions to ask: Did you have the appropriate testing participants, and did you provide them with relevant context? Were the prototypes understandable, and did they align with the testing parameters? Were the potential solutions strong enough, or do more ideas need to be generated? Is it possible that the business challenge wasn't defined clearly enough?

Backing up in the design-thinking process is frustrating, but it doesn't need to be disheartening. No one gets the solution correct the first time, every time. Consider this: prior to the design-thinking process, your arsenal of weapons for solving a business challenge consisted of gut instinct, assumptions, and a modest amount of data. At the end of the design thinking process, you have nearly the opposite—a lot of data, clarity of purpose, and a little bit of gut instinct to add some flavor.

# Summary

We started our review of design thinking at the 30,000-foot level, and then dove deeper into its five distinct phases: Understand, Define, Ideate, Prototype, and Test. We reviewed the importance of understanding what your business challenge truly entails. We covered how to specifically define the business challenge so you can ideate with purpose. And we discussed the need for prototypes and testing to help ensure that you are on a path toward a viable business solution.

You may feel as though you're drinking from a fire hose; this is a lot of information to consume at once. Furthermore, I'm asking you to internalize this information using a way of thinking with which you may not yet be comfortable. If you are feeling unsure about how to proceed with design thinking, don't worry. It's normal, and I've been there. As with any new undertaking, practice and familiarity will lead to confidence.

The following chapters will explain how to implement design thinking in specific business scenarios, with examples and special tips to help you integrate it into your own business. By the end, you will know yourself to be a designer.

# The Role of Research in Design Thinking

## Don't Assume: Ask!

Data can be intimidating, elusive, and enlightening. Obtaining it, specifically taking the time to conduct meaningful research, can seem like an obstacle to progress. It's not. Research facilitates progress's emergence from the primordial soup of data so it can begin to take shape and form a solution.

When faced with a business challenge and using design thinking to help develop a solution to the challenge, you need research.

Your initial reaction is probably one or more of these three:

- I don't have time for research.
- I don't have the budget for research.
- I don't have the patience for research.

Sadly, most small businesses and entrepreneurs will skimp on research when time and budget are perceived issues. In this chapter, I demonstrate that you do have the time, budget, and patience for research, and that research is an absolute imperative in design thinking to keep you from chasing rabbits down trails that lead to nowhere.

# Design Thinking Research Is Different

Research in the design thinking context is not the static search we employed during late nights in the library or online hunting for facts to support our theses. It is not simply a means to an end. In design thinking research is an inquisitive quest for insights and perspectives that constantly evolves and truly has no end. It is purposeful in its pursuit of information, and it uses the results to inform business decisions.

Research in design thinking takes the form of asking a question—which can be done in numerous ways—and documenting the answer. Research doesn't need to be large-scale quantitative surveys that undergo regressive analysis to arrive at actionable answers. (Thank goodness, because how many entrepreneurs and small-business owners can conduct regressive analysis? Not I.) Nor does design thinking research need involve expensive, elaborate, in-depth, long-term qualitative studies.

---

**Note**   Design thinking research is purposeful, affordable, and actionable. Why assume when you can know?

---

Granted, design thinking research certainly has the capacity to be as elaborate as your budget and time will allow. Most notably, it can be inexpensive, simple, and scalable. What it fundamentally cannot be is omitted.

# Quantitative versus Qualitative

For our discussion, we classify research into two categories: quantitative and qualitative, often referred to as "quant" and "qual." Each has its own strengths and weaknesses; neither is superior to the other. There are some business cases in which it is perfectly acceptable to conduct only one of the two research categories, but these are few and far between. I recommend that you refrain from putting all of your research eggs into one category's basket, because a balanced approach will be more informative and more likely to reveal a broader scope of opportunity to develop solutions to your business challenge. Eschewing one type for the other will not save you any time or money, so plan for both.

## The "Quant"

Quantitative research is characterized by its focus on measurable data that can be extrapolated and applied to a population greater than the one tested. It is commonly used to gather demographic data, measure opinion using a predefined scale, and collect customer or user behavioral data. Surveys are the poster children of quantitative research because they can be constructed, distributed, and evaluated easily. Whether delivered online, via telephone, or through regular mail, surveys collect data in limited categories using predominantly closed questions. The length of a quantitative survey typically is dictated by what data are known currently and what data need to be collected to complete the desired data set.

Quantitative data can also be gathered through web analytics (page views, original visitors, click-throughs, etc.), point-of-sale software, online polls, and customer feedback forms.

## The "Qual"

Qualitative research is characterized by its exploratory nature. It is more about depth than breadth, and results are not as easily extrapolated to larger populations. However, the information collected is rich in a level of detail and nuance that isn't possible in quantitative research. The stereo-typed image of qualitative data is the focus group. Despite focus groups being characterized and parodied in popular media, this interview method is valuable because it provides an opportunity for deeper exploration into the consumer's opinions, purchasing behavior, and lifestyle factors that might influence that behavior. The nature of the topic being researched will dic-tate the type and size of group and the demeanor of the interview. If you are discussing potty training with a group of young parents, the questions will likely be light and humorous and the atmosphere convivial. However, if you are discussing financial investments and retirement funds, the questions will take a more serious tone, and the atmosphere will likely reflect that.

Other means of gathering qualitative data include one-on-one interviews, in-store interceptions (in which a shopper is interrupted briefly to be asked questions about their immediate purchasing decisions), and obser-vation of your potential consumers in their natural habitats.

## The Four Roles of Research

Research in design thinking plays the roles of Equalizer, Archeologist, Interpreter, and Devil's Advocate. Research levels the knowledge field and puts all of your team members on the same page, understanding your business challenge from the same data set. It helps uncover the roots of the challenge so you don't take it simply at face value. It translates the needs and wants of the customer into insights on which you can take action. It can be the tempered balance to enthusiasm that shines a cau-tionary light on a solution's potential flaws.

# The Equalizer

Surveys are the ideal equalizer in design thinking research, because they can provide a measured overview of the market, the competitive environment, customer demographics, purchasing patterns, and similar broad-scope views that give the lay of the land. Surveys essentially level the playing field for businesses because they can be conducted cheaply and quickly and can be quite pointed in their questions.

If you find yourself working in a vacuum with no known data, surveys can remedy that situation. You can gather even the most basic of data—like customer names. Consider this scenario: you have a new formula for laundry detergent that minimizes environmental impact without sacrificing the perceived level of cleanliness that customers expect. You have plenty of industry data, and perhaps even consumer data harvested from several markets across the country. However, you haven't launched your product yet, so you have zero customer data unique to you. You have a general idea of your target customer based on the existing information you gathered, but you want to ask specific questions to discover who among the vast universe of people who do laundry in your launch markets would choose your new greener, but slightly more expensive product instead of their usual choice.

---

**Tip**   You don't have to work in a data vacuum. Use surveys to gather even the most basic information from customers to jump-start your research.

---

You can distribute a survey to a population that looks like your general target customer and collect data from scratch. That data set might include questions about income, family size, geographic region, current product preference, frequency of use, purchase behavior, and opinions about the environment. Once the data are collected and analyzed, you'll be able to identify the consumer groups most likely to make the switch to your product. The outcome could read something like this: "Women age thirty to forty-five with children living at home, with an annual household income of more than $60,000 who buy laundry detergent at least once every six to eight weeks, and who are somewhat or very concerned about the environment." You now have a well-defined, specific consumer segment—supported by data!—to whom you can begin to market.

Alternatively, you may have some consumer data to work with but need more details. For established businesses with modest data capture capabilities, this is common. You may have some customer contact details and past purchase history, but not much more. In that case, the scenario may look like this: you are an automobile dealer, and during the process of selling a vehicle, you collect age, race, marital status, home ownership status, income level, and credit score data. If you accepted a trade-in vehicle for the new purchase, you also gathered data on the make, model, and year of that vehicle. At this point, you have a fairly detailed picture of your customer, but you want to know more.

After the purchase, you distribute a brief survey—via mail or email—that asks the customer additional questions about his or her experience at your business (a potential indicator of repeat or word-of-mouth referral business), what other dealers they visited and/or considered before making the purchase (a measurement of who they perceive the company's competitors to be), and how many other vehicles they own (an indicator of consumption capacity for this type of purchase).

All of these data are merged with the data collected during the vehicle purchase. Combined, it goes into your database of customers, which now contains much more robust content to better inform and direct your company's leaders when they begin to explore new business opportunities or face new challenges.

## The Archeologist

Qualitative research, at least in my mind, resembles the romanticized image of the archaeologist, that intrepid explorer bent on unearthing hidden treasures, truths, and beliefs that can shed light on how and why we do what we do as humans and consumers. Think about it: somewhere, someone conducted some research among a group of consumers a lot like you to determine what type of teapot they would most prefer to purchase. Then they used the data from that research to design precisely that type of teapot.

I find qualitative research fascinating, highly valuable, and eminently important to the design-thinking process. My preferred means of qualitative exploration are focus groups and customer intercepts. Those are the qualitative research methods we explore next.

Before we jump into the details of how to conduct this type of research, it's good to note that collecting the insights revealed during either of these activities are best recorded with video and supplemented with written notes. Fortunately, you aren't recording for a screening at the Sundance Film Festival, so the quality of your video doesn't have to be anything more than comprehensible. Using a video app on your smart phone is sufficient. As mentioned in the previous chapter, it is imperative to have your participants agree to recording their likeness and signing a waiver to that effect. Logistically, getting a waiver signed during a customer intercept might be a hassle, but it is always better to err on the side of caution and cover your bases.

## Customer Intercepts

Customer intercepts are a quick, somewhat informal way to get brief answers to limited questions that are relative to what a customer is doing in real time. To conduct these, you truly intercept customers during their activity—be it shopping for or using the product or service for which you are conducting research. Therefore, the way you approach customers is critical, as is the brevity of your interaction with them. As you are considering the questions you want to ask customers and the way you will approach them, put yourself in their shoes. Construct the intercept in such a way that if you were the customer, you would willingly answer a few questions posed by a stranger.

Because our culture propagates a distrust of strangers, your countenance and body language are important in getting a response. Your actions speak louder than words here. For successful customer intercepts, the interviewer should be open, friendly, curious, approachable, and somewhat extroverted without coming across as overbearing or obnoxious. I encourage senior leadership to conduct interviews when possible, as they get the opportunity to hear the customer feedback firsthand. However, anyone on your team who matches this description would be a good choice as an interviewer.

Before conducting any intercepts, determine the questions for which you need answers. You'll want to identify no more than two main questions, with a follow-up question for each. That's it—short and sweet. You should also think through questions that might be asked of you by the customer and formulate your answers. If your interviewer is not involved with determining the questions, be sure he or she understands what information you want to glean from this process so they are well informed going into the activity.

Next, determine where these intercepts will happen. For locations anywhere other than your own place of business, you'll need to secure permission from the appropriate people, like store managers. If you plan to conduct your intercepts in public spaces, take the time to investigate whether you need permits or permission from local authorities. Once you have your location, schedule dates and times during which you are most likely to encounter the type of customers you want to interview. Don't just go to where your customers are, go *when* they are there.

Let's illustrate all of this customer intercept information with an example.

> You operate a small business that provides locally produced, artisanal cheese using milk from grass-fed, free-ranging goats on your small farm just outside of the city. Your cheese is distributed through a regional grocery retailer and is shelved alongside three national brands and two other local brands. You want to conduct

customer intercepts to better understand the decision-making process buyers go through when selecting goat cheese. Your interviewer is placed near enough to the cheese case to be able to see what cheese is selected but not so close that he or she is obtrusive. Once a customer selects a package of goat cheese—regardless of the brand selected—your interviewer will then approach him or her. She should introduce herself and indicate that she is interviewing customers about their preferences in cheese. She should not share the brand of the cheese for which she is conducting the interviews unless specifically asked by the customer. Sharing that information up front could influence the customer's answers, as most people do not want speak ill of a brand directly to a brand's representative.

After the introduction, your interviewer should inform the customer that his answers are being recorded for research reference only and obtains the customer's verbal permission (if the interview is being recorded). Then the questions can begin. In this scenario, the lead question could be "Why did you select that brand of goat cheese?" If the customer's answer is not specific, for example, "I don't know," the follow-up should be more direct, such as, "Did you find the packaging more appealing than the others? Or did you select the product based on the price?" Your second main question could be about the product being locally produced and the importance that fact did or did not play in the customer's choice. If the customer didn't select your brand, your interviewer could inquire about what product features would prompt him to switch to your brand. At this point, the interviewer is done and should thank the customer for their help. The customer may engage your interviewer in conversation, and that is fine as long as your interviewer isn't missing opportunities to speak to other customers.

## Focus Groups

Focus groups are the stuff of which advertising legends are made. The focus group as portrayed in television and film—think *Mad Men*—is a stereotype of the experience. Although there is always some kernel of truth in a stereotype, focus groups don't have to be expensive, complicated, or dramatic. They won't make or break a product or service. They will, however, provide the opportunity to explore, somewhat in depth, the "why" behind customer behavior.

Marketing strategist and former psychologist George Silverman explains focus groups like this:

> The open-ended interaction of focus groups leads to stimulation of thoughts and emotions, the revelation of material which is not ordinarily forthcoming in an individual interview, the examination of how people in various roles interact, and the observation of important behavior.[1]

The open-ended nature of focus groups make the research technique appealing. They are inherently exploratory, framed by two or more investigative, collaborative activities through which a moderator guides the group to reveal relevant insights from the customers' perspectives. Focus groups are best used when more detailed, nuanced information is needed or when the customer's decision-making process is complicated. Health care and finance are prime examples of industries that benefit from focus group research when developing their products and services.

The primary ingredient for focus groups—with the exception of target customers—is the moderator. I consider personality to be critical when selecting a moderator. He or she must be able to make connections with the focus group participants and quickly build a comfortable rapport, yet maintain enough distance and control to keep the group on task. The moderator is not a part of the group but is their guide. I consider moderating a group to be similar to supervising other people's children: the moderator is friendly, likable, and engaging, but always in control. If you have the opportunity to contract with an independent moderator, I encourage you to do so. Conducting a focus group requires a certain amount of skill, finesse, and experience. If you don't have a budget for a moderator, don't let that be a barrier to using focus groups to your advantage. With a little studying and preparation, you could lead the group yourself. It's not ideal, but it can be done.

The second critical component for a focus group is the moderator's guide. This is a written document that outlines how the group will spend its time together. If an independent moderator is used, the guide will likely contain granular detail, including scripted copy for the moderator's welcome, introduction, instructions, and so on, as an added benefit to you, the client. An independent moderator will want to ensure that you are informed of all the focus group procedures. If you are serving as your own moderator, the guide should provide as much detail as you need to stay focused and communicate clearly with the group. The moderator's guide is a document for the moderator's own use, so it doesn't need to be pretty, just thorough.

---

[1] George Silverman, "How to Get Beneath the Surface in Focus Groups," http://mnav.com/focus-group-center/bensurf-htm/.

With a clear understanding of how the focus group will flow and having selected a moderator, it's time to recruit participants. I have moderated groups with as many as twelve participants and as few as three. My ideal focus group is no fewer than three but no more than six. There is no magic to that number; I find the group size manageable for a moderator and engaging for a participant. If you have a group larger than ten, you run the risk of group think (the natural tendency of groups to gravitate toward a harmonious outcome while forsaking their individual opinions) taking hold and skewing your results.

The participants you invite to the focus group should reflect the characteristics of your target market as closely as possible. Going back to our goat cheese example, if the primary target market for your product is women, ages thirty to fifty, who have children, with household incomes of more than $60,000 a year, and who exercise three or more times a week, then your focus group should consist of that same type of person. Furthermore, you should organize your focus group participants so that the group is as homogeneous as possible, for example, stay-at-home moms with stay-at-home moms, working moms with working moms. By grouping like participants together, you help create rapport among the group, and they can build on one another's answers and thoughts. You can recruit focus group participants in many ways, the most popular and cost-effective of which include social media, your personal and professional networks, and word-of-mouth referrals.

Whether you've selected an independent moderator or have taken on that role yourself, it is extremely valuable to summarize the focus group's proceedings, the insights learned, the "take-aways," and their implications within a day or two after the focus group is completed. (If you've worked with a moderator, a summary report should be a part of the scope of work for which you contracted him or her.) Summarizing the experience and insights soon after the focus group will help you not only document what you saw and heard, but also capture thoughts and impressions that you may not have noted while the focus group was under way.

## The Interpreter

There is a wealth of inquiry-driven research tools that can complement focus groups or stand alone. These tools serve as interpreters of customer insight and are particularly beneficial in providing added clarity to customers' responses to the questions asked. Without a doubt, the majority of these tools resemble games, and many of them are captured in a wonderful encyclopedic resource called *Gamestorming*, written by Sunni Brown, David Grey, and James Macanufo. Rather than regurgitating their work, I focus on two of my go-to interpreter tools that generate a lot of discussion among research participants and yield a lot of insight.

## Photo Sort

If a picture is worth a thousand words, you should use them to your research advantage. They are especially advantageous if you're research- ing areas of consumer behavior rooted in deep-seated emotions, or nebu- lous topics such as brand personality. The photo sort activity is perfect for use in small focus groups or individual interviews.

The images used in the photo sort exercise are generally sourced from magazines and the Internet, and the process of gathering the images is incredibly contemplative, prompting the researcher to think through all aspects of the exercise and the intended outcomes. Images pulled from magazines and the Internet are protected by copyright laws; you shouldn't run into any legal issues with using them because you will use them for noncommercial purposes, as I am describing here.

In practical terms, you'll want to use images that are in color, at least as large as your palm, and on a white background. If you have to cut out an image from a magazine and glue it to a sheet of white paper, do it. If you will be using the images with some frequency, perhaps with multiple groups of research participants, then you would benefit from having them laminated at your nearest copy shop so they will be more durable.

How, exactly, do you go about selecting images to use in this exercise? It is entirely dependent on the topic being researched. The key is that each image represents an emotion in some way. If you can find images that rep- resent emotions *and* contain people who represent your target market, then all the better! (Those can be difficult to find, though.)

At this point, the photo sort activity may seem a bit vague, so let's con- sider this example: a financial services firm wants to use the photo sort activity in a focus group that will be discussing customers' perceptions of investing money. The insights derived from the photo sort activity will help direct the firm in developing new investment products and commu- nicating their benefits effectively to their target customer: men age forty- five and older, married or divorced with children, and with household incomes of more than $75,000. Before sourcing the images, you and your research team (whoever you've tapped to help you) need to brainstorm a list of emotions or emotional states that your target customer might experience in connection with investing money. Some of those could be fear, a sense of being overwhelmed, confident, tentative, procrastinating, empowered, and disengaged.

Once you have your list of emotions, the search for images begins. Major search engines, such as Google, allow you to search for images by keyword, for example "confident" or "unsure." You can also use photo-sharing sites as a resource. You will get thousands of results, so finding the images isn't the challenge. Selecting them is. Put yourself in your target customer's mindset when you review the images and try to determine what will resonate. Your goal is to compile a collection of diverse but representative images that reflect your list of emotions and emotional states.

---

■ **Tip**   Don't wait to build your image library. Whenever you come across an interesting or iconic image in your daily consumption of news and information, save it!

---

With your images selected and your focus group in place, the activity begins. Using the financial services example, you or your moderator is working with a group of five men who mirror your target consumer. With the array of images spread out in the center of the table, in front of the focus group participants, you ask the question, "Which of these images represents how you feel when you think about making financial investments?" The participants sift through the images and select as many as they like. The obvious follow-up question to each participant is "Why?" Be sure to allow each person time to explain his perspective and why he chose the image or images he did.

Documenting this activity, and capturing the insights revealed, is much like documenting any focus group session: audio and video recording is ideal, with additional written notes as needed.

## Dot Voting

When researching opinion on existing products or services or perspectives on the customer experience, the Dot Voting exercise is an excellent choice. It is a good activity for gleaning insights from larger groups. This activity is like a visual manifestation of the 1–10 point rating means of measurement, and that visualization can spark wonderfully rich discussion. The activity itself is incredibly easy to conduct, which makes it universally appealing.

Display a poster along one wall in which a continuum of opinion can be represented, with the least positive response on the left endpoint and the most positive response on the right endpoint. It's helpful to provide some points of measurement along the continuum to give your participants guideposts. Consider marking the center of the continuum or marking the quarters. I recommend not going as far as to mark each guidepost, 1 through 10, on the continuum. You want the continuum to be somewhat flexible in its interpretation, save for the center or quarter marks you provided.

Give each participant small round stickers—the kind you find in office supply stores that are typically in primary colors—in enough quantity to answer each of the questions you'll be posing, with one sticker representing one answer. In the financial services example, the moderator might ask the participants, "On a range from 1 to 10, where 1 is 'least important' and 10 is 'most important,' how important are your friends' or families' recommendations regarding investment decisions?" Then have each of your participants answer by placing a sticker along the continuum at a place that represents the importance of those recommendations. Once everyone has placed a dot, you can ask if anyone would like to share why they answered the way they did. Then, move on to the next question.

To help you interpret the results, assign each question a specific color of dot for the answer. At a glance, you'll be able to differentiate the answers by topic. To use the financial services example again, ask your participants, "How important is mobile banking?" The participants respond by placing a blue sticker on the poster along the continuum. Next, you ask, "How important are printed monthly statements?" and the participants answer, but this time with a yellow dot, and so on. What if you have more questions than you do colored dots? You can achieve the same outcome using markers.

The best way to document the Dot Voting activity is twofold. First, observe the participants' behavior and take written notes. More important, the second means of documentation is the culminating result of the activity: the poster. A tangible document in this context is generally referred to as an artifact, and it's a wonderful representation of the activity. Save it!

# The Devil's Advocate

Whereas the previous research tools and activities are focused on providing feedback and revealing opportunities for the researcher, the tools that I classify as devil's advocates are used to try and find gaps, reveal weaknesses, and generally question all assumptions associated with the product, service, or idea at the center of the research. These activities add balance to qualitative research efforts.

## The 5 Whys

My all-time favorite devil's advocate tool is called The 5 Whys. You'll feel like a toddler during the process as you ask "Why" at least five times, but trust me: it reveals some great insights. The 5 Whys emerged as an effective problem-solving technique during Toyota's pursuit of innovative improvements in its manufacturing process. Used in either a focus group setting or as a stand-alone exercise, The 5 Whys peel back the layers of perception and opinion to get to the core of what is being researched.

The process is simple. Start with a premise relative to what you are researching. In the financial services example, that premise could be "Our target customer wants to manage his investments online, without the assistance of an advisor." You ask your research participants, "Why?" The group discusses the possibilities of why and decides that the customer wants to manage his investments online because he wants the convenience that the online environment provides. You ask, "Why does he want convenience?" The group responds, and the process continues with a "Why?" followed by a group discussion and conclusion, and so on until collectively, all participating feels like they've uncovered the core issue and there is no more reasonable answers to "Why?" In the financial services example, ultimately the core could be that the customer doesn't want to pay a service fee that he assumes would be involved if he worked with an advisor.

The 5 Whys can be used in a focus group setting or online via a collaborative platform such as Basecamp[2] or even through an online survey service, such as Survey Monkey,[3] by using open-ended questions. Audio/video recording is the best choice for documenting the activity if you are conducting it live with a group. The data capture from conducting the activity in an online format is sufficient documentation, as it produces an artifact that can be saved and referred to repeatedly.

---

▨ **Caution**   Devil's advocate activities and tools can easily take on a negative tone and turn into gripe sessions. Be alert and ready to redirect the conversation to be more productive.

---

## Cannonball

Another excellent devil's advocate tool is called Cannonball, the goal of which is to "punch holes" in the idea, product, service, or process being researched. This tool is best used in a group setting with a moderator leading the discussion. Because participants are often shy at the beginning of the activity, they typically will punch holes gently, couching their thoughts as tentative suggestions. Don't let that hesitation fool you; this activity can easily accelerate into a barrage of hole-punch attempts, which often leads into lively discussion and debate.

Once again returning to our financial services example, Cannonball might focus on punching holes in the website developed to answer the target customer's desire for convenience. Research participants might punch holes in the way the website functions, what services are available through the website, and the way a user has to navigate the website.

---

[2]http://basecamp.com/.
[3]http://www.surveymonkey.com/.

Using Cannonball comes with a cautionary disclaimer: the moderator needs to understand that the discussion could easily turn negative in tone, and he or she needs to be prepared to redirect the conversation or reset the tone when necessary to keep the activity productive.

# Summary

Research helps eliminate the dangers inherent in making assumptions, which can be detrimental to your success. Design thinking research methods—both qualitative and quantitative—are affordable, accessible, and incredibly user-friendly, so you have no reason to skimp on it. The bottom line is that any of these research activities are frameworks for asking questions and getting answers that you can leverage to help you succeed. Remember, the only dumb question is the one not asked.

# Designing a Business Strategy

## Get Down to Business

A business strategy is created to outline purposefully the path a business must take to achieve its desired outcomes. Behind your business strategy is a series of deliberate, data-driven decisions about markets, products, and services. It also involves your organization's culture, from which your business goals, decision-making processes, and measurements of success evolve. When described this way, business strategy sounds energizing, dynamic, and meaningful. So why is it that the majority of business strategies appear constrained, confused, and stagnant?

I place the blame squarely on the lack of design thinking, which should be brought to bear during the strategic planning process. The roots of design thinking are empathy, purpose, and adaptability, and working with design thinking principles is inherently dynamic. It would follow, then, that if you apply design thinking principles when developing your business strategy, it will be dynamic, flexible, and effective.

## A Strategy Is Born

It's exciting to see a business opportunity, and instinctively we want to rush to take advantage of it before anyone else does. In that rush, we gloss right over the due diligence needed to develop a sound business strategy and a viable business model. Once we're neck deep in our business operations without those guides, we often realize that we have no clear vision for what we're doing or where we want to go. Growth stalls, operations hit a tailspin, and we might even panic a bit. To avoid that downward spiral, we need to harness the excitement and channel its energy into smart, purposeful planning.

---

▓ **Tip**   Clearly define your business opportunity with language everyone can understand. This should be a jargon-free zone.

---

The first, most critical step is to define clearly the business opportunity. For the purpose of this book, I'm going to assume that you are familiar with SWOT (Strengths, Weaknesses, Opportunities, Threats) analyses and assessing the competitive landscape, two common and important tools used for identifying and articulating business opportunities. If you need a refresher or are starting from square one, an Internet search of those terms will yield thousands of useful results. My purpose is to introduce you to—and encourage your use of—design thinking tools that will add depth and additional insight as you develop and define your business strategy.

Conduct your SWOT and competitive analyses first, because they will give you the foundation of information on which you can build your strategy. With those complete and in hand, you'll be prepared to introduce the following three design thinking tools into your business strategy planning: Circles of Influence, Context Map, and Stakeholder Visioning. These tools will give you insight from three critical perspectives:

1.   Yourself and your own network,

2.   The world outside of your business and its influences, and

3.   The key stakeholder groups involved in your venture.

The information these tools yield is laced with opinion, and that is okay. It balances the data-driven information in your SWOT and competitive analyses.

# Circles of Influence

We most often hear the phrase "circles of influence" in a persuasive context, such as sales or politics. For our purposes, the context is support and development of your business (Figure 3-1). The root of the Circles of Influence exercise lies in tapping into your personal, professional, and extended networks, identifying additional connections, and leveraging them to help you explore new markets, evaluate products and services, reach new customers, and more.

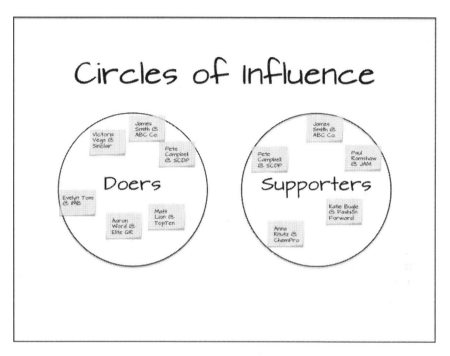

**Figure 3-1.** Circles of Influence activity diagram

If you are a sole proprietor, you can conduct the Circles of Influence activity on your own, but I encourage you to include others—close friends, your spouse, trusted colleagues, and mentors are good choices—but no more than four people. If you have an established leadership team that is larger than five people (you plus four others), you could consider working through this activity with a larger group, but you'll need to be diligent in keeping everyone focused and productive to avoid the "too many cooks in the kitchen" outcome.

As with all design thinking tools, Circles of Influence is best done through a visual exercise, but not just a boring list of whom you know. It is very hard to uncover connections in such a linear way. Use a dry erase board, a flip chart or poster board, or some other large surface on which you can write. Write your goal or purpose across the top, for example, "Launch our product with three companies of no more than 100 employees as a beta test." Be as specific as you can.

Under your goal statement, draw two large circles, leaving enough room between and around them to allow for written notes. Using a different color of ink for each circle is visually stimulating but not critical. In the center of left circle, write "Doers"; in the center of the right circle, write "Supporters." Give your participants, including yourself, a stack of sticky notes (the best office supply item ever). Give each person a different color pad of stickies, which will be helpful in understanding the dynamics of potential connections.

Starting with the Doers circle, have the group think of people they know who can provide specific, task-oriented help to achieve your goal. Each person needs to be named specifically—"James Smith in human resources at Company ABC" versus "someone in human resources at Company ABC." As each participant in your group thinks of a doer, he or she writes the doer's name on a sticky note and places it in the Doers circle. Once the group has thought of everyone possible, they collectively evaluate and discuss how connecting with each doer would be advantageous. Would the connection be mutually beneficial? Does the person know other potentially helpful people with whom your team could connect? Where can you plug these contacts into your strategic approach so you can get closer to accomplishing your goal?

Work together to identify whom to speak with first from the Doers circle. Who is the easiest person to talk to with the best return? Take notes during discussion so you don't lose any of these details, or better yet, audio or video record it as you would a focus group.

Now move on to the Supporters circle and follow the same process with specificity in naming the people who belong in that circle, such as "Anna Knutz with ChemPro." The difference between the Doers and Supporters circles is subtle but distinct: the people in the Supporters circle might not be able to do something specific to benefit your business strategy, but they provide thought leadership, support, enthusiasm, and a willingness to go the extra mile for you if asked.

Not everyone in the circles will provide value in the way you hope, and that's all right. Focus on the successes. In this example, perhaps it turns out that James Smith was delighted to be a beta tester, and Anna Knutz provided wise counsel that kept you on track.

---

**Tip**   During the Circle of Influencers activity, don't forget to look for people who belong to both circles. They are incredibly valuable connections because they can assist with something specific as well as provide support.

---

# Context Map

For the majority of us, when we are working on a challenging situation—and developing a business strategy certainly qualifies as challenging—it is truly difficult to see the bigger picture. We see the details we are most concerned with and miss others entirely. The cliché, "You can't see the forest for the trees" is the perfect descriptor.

Dave Gray, coauthor of *Gamestorming*,[1] has said, "We don't truly have a good grasp of a situation until we see it in a fuller context." The Context Map activity is designed to provide that bigger context. It is based on the premise that once you have a larger, systemic view of the environment in which your business is operating, you'll be better prepared to plan for and anticipate business and market needs at a larger scale.

The Context Map activity is interactive and requires some advance preparation on your part to get the most out of it. The group will drive the contributions and final outcome of the activity, but as the leader, you'll be responsible for spurring them along with relevant and thought-provoking questions. The goal is to describe the external environment in as much detail as possible, with the intent that the group can respond proactively, rather than reactively. The context map will help your team see the forest, not just the trees.

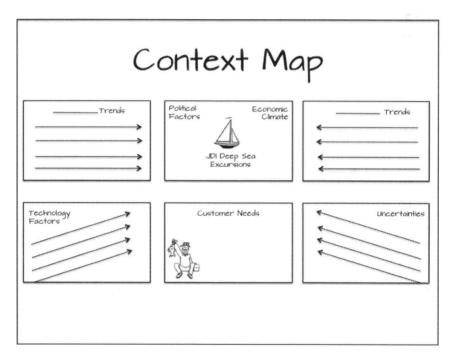

**Figure 3-2.** Context Map activity diagram

---

▧ **Tip**   Consider the Trends section as "square one," and start developing your context map from there.

---

[1]Dave Gray, Sunni Brown, and James Macanufo, *Gamestorming* (O'Reilly Media, 2010), p. 84.

The Context Map exercise always begins with an outline of current trends. The other sections of the map can be completed in any order. Rather than directing the group, I recommend you let them dictate the order after the Trends sections are completed and pay attention to the workflow. The areas that generate more content are fair indicators of where the team's focus and energy lie. Occasionally, the conversation drifts into analyzing the internal context—what's happening within your organization—so you may find it necessary to redirect the conversation. Remember, the Context Map exercise is best used for external exploration.

You'll need flip-chart paper, markers, and an expanse of wall for this activity. You can draw the necessary elements, which are described in more detail next, on the flip chart ahead of time and then post it on the wall, or post the paper first and then draw—whichever is easier for you. For the purpose of explanation, let's assume you are posting the paper first and then drawing.

Post six large sheets of paper on the wall so you have two rows of three columns. In the center of the top middle sheet, draw something that represents your business, for example, a place setting if you own a restaurant or a computer if you own a software company. It doesn't have to be elaborate. Then, label the picture appropriately with your company name (which helps if your drawing skills are marginal). On that same piece of paper, in the upper left corner, write "Political Factors." In the upper right corner, write "Economic Climate."

On the top left and top right sheets of paper, draw several long arrows pointing toward the center sheet, leaving enough room between them to add notes later. Label these sheets "_____ Trends," leaving the blank empty. Later in the activity, you'll name the trends. On the bottom left sheet, draw more arrows (again, with space in between), this time pointing up and to the right toward the top middle sheet. Label this sheet "Technology Factors."

On the bottom middle sheet, draw an image that represents your primary customer and label the sheet "Customer Needs." If you have more than one customer group you want to explore in this activity, add an additional sheet below that one and draw something representative of that second group. Don't include more than two customer groups in the context map, or the activity will get unwieldy.

On the bottom right sheet, draw arrows pointing up and to the left toward the top middle sheet, and label that sheet "Uncertainties."

Now you're ready to bring in your team and get started. Introduce the Context Map activity and explain its purpose: to help the team define and understand the bigger picture in which the business functions. Start with the Trends sections and have the team contribute the content while you add their comments to the sheet. Once the team feels the current trends have all been captured, move on to another section, but let them choose which one.

Follow the same process—contributing content and comments—for the remaining sections, one at a time, until they are all complete.

Using the illustrated example of JDI Deep Sea Excursions, Trends might include statements such as "25 percent increase in fishing gear sales in the last year," "Families spending more time on outdoor activities," and "Self-sustaining food movement = more gardens … more fishing?" Political Factors for JDI may include legislation that restricts fishing in particular areas or lobbying groups that actively campaign against leisure fishing at sea. The economic climate might include the rising cost of fuel and the increased cost of permits.

The Technology Factors section for JDI could include needing a stronger presence on the Internet or investing in developing technology to improve locating schools of fish. For the Customer Needs section, JDI may identify their primary customers as males above age twenty-five and list among its needs the desire to be able to book an excursion online. In the Uncertainties section, JDI will capture factors affecting its business that are still unclear, which could be pending legislation that will severely limit the number of fish allowed to be caught or how much the cost of fuel will rise.

Once all of the sections are complete, go back to Trends and review the team's original contributions in the context of the completed map. Do any of those identified trends need to change? Are they all on point? For example, if your team isn't confident that the self-sustaining food movement has exerted enough influence in the market to affect your business, they may choose to remove that trend from the map. Make any adaptations as necessary and then, as a team, come up with a description for those trends in the blank space.

To close the Context Map activity, lead the group through a summary discussion of what occurred and solicit feedback along the lines of insights, a ha! moments, and areas that need further exploration. The last step is to agree as a group that the context map is the most accurate representation of the environment in which the business is operating. I often encourage teams to leave the context map posted for several days following the activity for reinforcement, as long as it can be posted in an area away from clients, vendors, and potential competitors.

## Stakeholder Visioning

Every business has multiple groups of stakeholders who have varying degrees of vested interest in its success and perspectives on what that success looks like. Stakeholder Visioning, when used in developing a business strategy, provides a 360-degree review of your business from the multiple perspectives of your stakeholders. It also gives the participants an opportunity to relate intuitive knowledge and subject matter expertise. With these multiple perspectives, you can explore possible futures and uncover potential gaps that could impede success.

Divide your team and assign them to a stakeholder group that they will represent during the activity. You'll have at least two groups: customers and employees. Depending on the nature of your business, you may want to include others, such as vendors, community members, shareholders, investors, or mentors. Have them sit together in their new groups, and consider having each participant wear a nametag with their group name on it, for example, "Customer," or in some other way indicate each group so that participants are clearly identified and no one gets confused.

Ask them to step into their roles and imagine your business—and their involvement in it—five years in the future. What will the business be like? What will they value as a group? What trends do they think will have emerged? What do they think the competitive environment be like? What specifically will have changed over those five years? Have the participants write their responses on sticky notes, one thought per note. If it helps them communicate their ideas better, than can illustrate the notes, as well. Then have each group present their perspectives. For example, an employee might value increased profits and be concerned that the business may become less competitive in five years, whereas a vendor might value the opportunity to diversify its own business by working with yours and might see a potential permanent partnership in five years.

Once each stakeholder group has presented, ask the participants to step out of their roles and review the perspectives from their own points of view. Sort the sticky notes into common themes. Within those themes, have the team identify any opportunities that can be incorporated into your business strategy now to capitalize on future potential.

---

■ **Tip** If time allows, cycle through the Stakeholder Vision activity several times so that your team has the opportunity to adopt multiple roles.

---

# Summary

A sound business strategy is critical to success, and traditional means of planning a strategy are no longer sufficient. Developing a plan to keep your business viable and resilient in a volatile marketplace needs design thinking. When you add design thinking tools to the process, you can push your business strategy to be more robust and comprehensive.

# Designing Live Customer Experiences

## Maximizing "Face Time"

One of the more visible ways design thinking can be manifested is through live customer experiences, meaning the ways a customer interacts with your brand and business in person. In fact, now that the customer experience has become recognized as an important part of the success of a brand, a specialized marketing discipline has emerged: *experiential marketing*.

Experiential marketing allows customers to engage and interact with brands, products, and services in a sensory context, helping them connect with the brand in meaningful, personal ways. These personal interactions and the connections they build lead to informed purchasing decisions. Designing live customer experiences propels your brand beyond the narrative of the features of your product or service; customers experience the benefits firsthand.

You can leverage design thinking tools to create brand interactions with purpose and meaning, and to do that effectively, you must be able to empathize with your customer. Quite simply, if you were your customer, what would your expectations for your brand be? How would you want to interact with your brand and business? What would you want to derive from that interaction? What would you want to feel afterward?

From the physical space your brand occupies to customer service processes to employee training, every touch point with a customer is an opportunity to showcase your brand, set the tone of the customer conversation, and build loyalty.

# Your Bricks-and-Mortar Location

If your business has a physical space—an office, warehouse, retail store, or open space—this is where a brand's first impressions are often made. Putting some thought into how your brand interacts with a customer in a physical space is particularly important for those businesses with revenue models that rely heavily on person-to-person transactions. Let's put this concept into personal terms as an example.

Imagine you are hosting someone very important at your home for dinner. Perhaps they are your future in-laws, your banker, the chairman of a nonprofit on whose board you serve, or a prospective new executive you are considering hiring. You want to put your best foot forward, right? You give your house a thorough cleaning, arrange freshly potted flowers on the front porch, set the table with your best china, and maybe even check to be sure your medicine cabinet doesn't contain anything questionable. We've all done this (or similar things) because we wanted our guests to feel welcome and comfortable, but also because we wanted to portray ourselves—our personal brand—in a certain light.

Now let's put this in business terms. Imagine you are hosting a potential customer for a meeting at your office, during which you hope to close a deal that will result in doubling your gross revenues for the fiscal year. Is your office designed to provide the type of experience with your brand that you want that customer to have? Or is your space somewhat haphazardly put together without any consideration of your brand?

If your physical space is a retail store, is it welcoming without being overwhelming? Is it designed to engage customers as they navigate the space? Is your team trained to provide a specific interpersonal experience for customers?

To evaluate your brand experience in terms of physical space, as honestly as possible, put yourself in your customers' shoes. Better yet, recruit a few of your leadership team and friends to join you and gather several perspectives. For illustrative purposes, I'll use a retailer as the first example, because I believe retail is one business sector with the most to gain when the live customer experience is designed.

Start evaluating from the parking lot: is the area clean, and does it feel safe? Is your entrance well marked, attractive, welcoming, and free of debris? These points seem basic, but they are essential and often overlooked.

---

**Tip** Don't give a trashy first impression. Make sure your parking lot or car park, sidewalks, and breezeways are clean and debris-free.

---

Next, evaluate the customers' experience when they arrive at your store. Do the interior design, merchandising, and product selection align with your brand? For example, if your business is a specialty running store and you've defined your brand as approachable, egalitarian, and friendly, does the interior of your store support that brand message with open spaces, welcoming but energizing colors, and places to sit? Does your product selection appeal to beginners as well as experienced runners? Does your merchandising and signage encourage the customer to explore your store? Is the lighting appealing and sufficient? If you have a music system, what's playing? I had a completely incongruous experience in a specialty running store in Scotland, in which the system was broadcasting country-and-western music with predominantly slow tempos not at all conducive to running. Rather than feeling energized, ready to run, and hyped up for new gear, I felt slower, more relaxed, and in no hurry to make a purchase—certainly not the customer experience the brand intended.

What if you have an office rather than a retail space? The approach is similar. Start from the parking lot and work your way inside. If your office is on an upper floor, take the elevator and perceive it through your customer's viewpoint. Is it too slow? Do the doors close too quickly (especially important if your customers tend to be older or physically challenged in some way)?

Once you arrive at your office, does your reception area or lobby reinforce your brand? For example, a conservative health care corporation may furnish its lobby in traditionally styled, dark wood furniture accented with oriental rugs and classic still-life painting reproductions. A cutting-edge architecture firm, on the other hand, may design its reception area with reclaimed materials, ultra-modern furnishings, and colorful, original artwork. If the physical setting of your reception or lobby is incongruous with your brand message or devoid of any attention to detail, then the customer experience is one of confusion and uncertainty, which is not the first impression you're counting on.

Carry this evaluative process throughout the public spaces of your office or retail space, and pay attention to detail. Restrooms, dressing rooms, conference rooms, and work areas are opportunities for reinforcing the experience you purposefully design. They are also where an experience that started off beautifully can deteriorate, sometimes irrevocably.

# Color Theory and You

*Color is important as the effects are instantaneous; for example blue connects the human mind to the universe and alleviates any sense of tight enclosure or claustrophobia that could occur in a windowless environment.*

—Leatrice Eiseman, director of the Eiseman Center for Color Information and Training[1]

Explanations of color theory are plentiful on the Internet, and you can find a much deeper history of its evolution and role in marketing, as well as behavioral science. Here I'll touch lightly on how color theory comes into play with regard to designing physical space, and color's effects on live customer experiences.

Simply put, color theory attempts to explain what feelings specific colors evoke and why. I say "attempt" because color is a highly subjective design element. The emotion a color evokes in one person could be markedly different in another. The reaction to color can be influenced by personal preference as well as cultural perspective.

---

■ **Tip** Avoid the tendency to design your office or store based on your personal preferences, especially when it comes to color. Put your brand's identity and personality before your own.

---

There are widely accepted generalities that you should consider when evaluating your physical space in terms of the customer experience and supporting your brand. You'll notice that some colors seem to evoke feelings that are quite different from each other, a result of how—and how much—the color is used in design.

## Warm Colors

Warm colors include red, yellow, and orange and generally convey passion, happiness, enthusiasm, and energy.

- Red, a primary color, and its various hues can be used to communicate power and passion, as well as danger. Brighter reds have more energy; muted, darker reds have more elegance.

---

[1]Personal conversation with author.

- Yellow, which is also a primary color, can be perceived as happy and hopeful, but also as cautious. Softer yellows convey a sense of calm, whereas darker yellows with a more golden hue can convey wealth or permanence.

- Orange is vibrant and energetic, and is often associated with vitality and movement. Orange garners attention in a way that is considered less aggressive than red.

# Cool Colors

Cool colors include blue, green, and purple, and they are considered calming, soothing, and less intense than their warm counterparts. Therefore, these colors and their various hues are frequently used to convey a sense of professionalism and maturity.

- Blue is most readily associated with calmness, responsibility, and peace, with darker hues conveying a greater sense of stability and strength while lighter hues feel refreshing.

- Green is the color of nature and almost universally conveys a sense of life, growth, new beginnings, and wealth. Brighter greens, incorporating a lot of yellow, are energizing and inspirational. Alternatively, darker greens that include more blue than yellow are seen as stable, solid, and reliable.

- Purple has long been associated with royalty, wealth, and spirituality. Darker, richer hues of purple convey wealth and regality. Lighter purples, such as lavender and lilac, are more commonly associated with spirituality and romance.

Color in a business's physical space can go a long way toward creating the type of environment—and by extension, a type of feeling—you want your customers to experience. In terms of your particular business, color should be used to reinforce your brand and its image. For example, a plant nursery would certainly lean toward using a lot of green—symbolizing nature, life, and growth—in its physical environment whether through the plants it stocks, paint and decorative elements, or both. However, a nursery may also want to punctuate its environment with yellow (happy) and orange (energy), both of which appear frequently in natural settings. Alternatively, a financial adviser might opt for shades of blue (professionalism) and purple (wealth).

If the colors in your physical space aren't aiding in creating the kind of experience you want for your customers—such as too much red in a psychologist's office or too much blue in the gym—don't despair. More often than not, a new paint color will put your space back on the right track. If painting isn't an option for you, or if a lot of your color comes from your furnishings, you still have alternatives. The psychologist with too much red in his office can temper that fire with cooler colors by incorporating a few accessories in shades of blue or purple. The gym owner could energize the workout environment with shades of orange or yellow.

# The Human Element

Truly, nothing can make or break a live customer experience than the human element—your team. You know this because you've experienced it firsthand in your own encounters with brands. I'm willing to bet that the businesses you frequent most deliver a customer experience that has made you feel welcomed, understood, appreciated, satisfied, or some combination of these. You shouldn't deliver anything less to your own customers. To ensure that great experience, you need to indoctrinate your team members. They need to be living, breathing representations of your brand with a commitment to the Golden Rule: treat others as you want to be treated. It works in life, and it works in commerce.

One of my favorite design thinking tools for training teams to create knock-'em-dead live customer experiences is the empathy map. Empathy makes the word go around smoothly; without it, we have misunderstanding and disruption. The empathy map tool leads teams through a process that helps them develop empathy for the customer, which leads teams to craft experiences that they—as the customer—would want.

## Create an Empathy Map

The goal of the empathy map in terms of customer experiences is to gain a deeper understanding of customers, and their wants, needs, and expectations with regard to their interaction with your team, business, and brand. I liken the process to the cliché of walking in someone else's shoes; the empathy map is the metaphorical pair of shoes. Creating an empathy map can be simple and completed in less than thirty minutes, which makes it a doable exercise to conduct during a staff meeting. It is the perfect place to start your team's training in designing customer experiences.

Ideally, you'll conduct the Empathy Map exercise with a team of no more than ten and no fewer than four. If you are a sole proprietor or a young start-up with a very small team, consider asking your spouse, a mentor, a friend, or any other trusted advisors and individuals to join you.

To start, you (or your moderator, if you choose to use one) will need a large whiteboard or flip chart and markers in at least two colors. In the center of the board, draw something that represents your customer. I often use the ubiquitous "Hello, my name is _____" name badge with "Your Customer" in the blank. It's easy to draw and everyone recognizes it (Figure 4-1). Across the top of the board, write out the topic you want to address in the exercise. In this case, it's "Our customer's experience in our store/office and with our team."

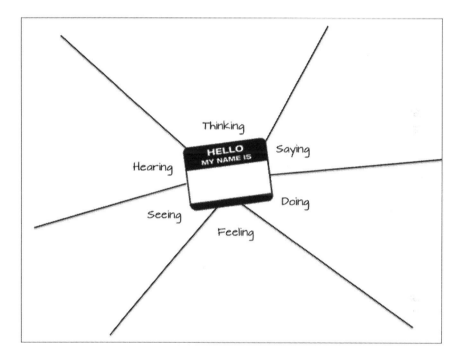

**Figure 4-1.** Empathy Map activity diagram

Then divide the remainder of your board into six sections, radiating out from the name badge image. Label the sections "Thinking," "Hearing," "Saying," "Doing," "Seeing," and "Feeling." Now it's time to put on those metaphorical shoes and start walking. Have everyone participating imagine him- or herself as your customer with the intent of populating the diagram with real sensory experiences from the customer's point of view.

You can start populating the diagram from any section, and the order in which you fill it in doesn't matter. In fact, you may find yourself and your team jumping among sections as the responses flow. Note the most common question from participants at the beginning of this exercise is "Are we saying what the customer is thinking/hearing/saying/doing/seeing/feeling *now*, or do we say what we *want* the customer to think/hear/say/do/see/feel?" This is an extremely valid question and begs for clarification.

In a perfect world, the team would stay focused on the customer's responses as they would be in the present. If those responses don't align with what the experience should be, address that separately with a different design thinking tool like Microscoping (see Chapter 7). However, the world isn't perfect and that singular focus on the "now" can be difficult to maintain. Rather than force the issue, I let groups respond in terms of both "now" and "want." This allows you to capitalize on the inevitable brainstorming around the customer experience that arises during the Empathy Map exercise. The key is to distinguish between the "now" and "want" by using different colors of ink. Be sure to include a key somewhere on the board that identifies which color is assigned to each type of response.

For the purposes of this example, I'll start with "thinking." Have your team consider what the customer is thinking during a live customer experience and write those thoughts in the diagram, using the terms and language your customer would use. Using the specialty running store as an example, the customer might be thinking, "I'm not sure what questions to ask," "This employee is really listening to me," "I feel comfortable in here even though I'm not a serious runner." Remember, the point of the exercise is to empathize with customers so you can design a live experience they will appreciate. Continue on in this manner through all of the senses until the diagram is complete.

Now that your empathy map is complete, you have a lens through which you can view your business, your operations, your staff's training, and your product and service offerings from your customer's perspective. Understanding the customer's perspective and adopting it as your own are invaluable as you move through the following design thinking exercises to design engaging, live customer experiences.

---

▓ **Note**    If in the process you find that you don't know as much about your customer as you thought, and you have gaps in your empathy map, that's okay. Now you'll know what areas in which you need more research to better understand your customer.

---

## Mapping the Customer Experience

Now that you better understand your customer after using the empathy map design thinking tool, what do you do with that knowledge? You design the live experience your customers most desire. The customer journey map (CJM) is a visual means by which you design how a customer interacts with your business and brand. Originally and still effectively used in service design, the CJM identifies all the touch points where a customer interacts with your business, including decision making and exit points, where delivering the optimum customer experience can be even more critical than at other points along the journey.

The objective with a CJM is to map a customer's experience with your business. Think of a game board with pathways and a definitive start and finish. Your map at the end of this exercise will look somewhat like a game board with descriptive detail in each space.

You'll need the usual design thinking materials for this exercise as you've used with others: a white board or flip chart, markers, and two colors of sticky notes.

---

**Tip**    If you haven't stocked up on markers, sticky notes, and flip charts yet, get thee to an office supply store. You'll be glad you did.

---

## Start at "Start"

As with every game—or process, adventure, or analysis—you have to start at the beginning. With a CJM, your starting place is the first point of contact your customer has with your business, and there could be several of them. Returning to the specialty running store example, the starting places for a customer's live experience are the store, the telephone, and online. You may be wondering how an online starting point can be a part of a live customer experience. Consider how often customers—including yourself—search online for directions to a store, look up a store's operating hours, or review products on a store's website prior to visiting the physical location. That activity leads to the live experience and is therefore important to the process.

To create your CJM, on the far left of your workspace (white board or flip chart page), start three rows or paths, with "Store," "Phone," and "Online" as your starting places. Be sure to leave a few inches of space between paths, so you have room to add sticky notes.

Next, pick one path to focus on. For our purposes, let's focus on the store path. The first step along the store path is entering the premises. Draw a square like you would see on a board game and label it "Enter." On one color of sticky notes, have your team write short descriptions of what the customer's experience is now on entering the store. For example, "Customer squints because there isn't enough light to see," or "The sightline is open, so the customer can see the whole store at a glance." On the other color of sticky notes, have your team write short descriptions of what you want the customer's experience to be: "Customer sees the latest merchandise on display," and "Customer hears the door chime, so he or she knows employees are aware that someone has walked in." If there are descriptions that fall into both now and want categories, great! You should write those descriptions on both colors of sticky notes and put them in their respective areas (Figure 4-2).

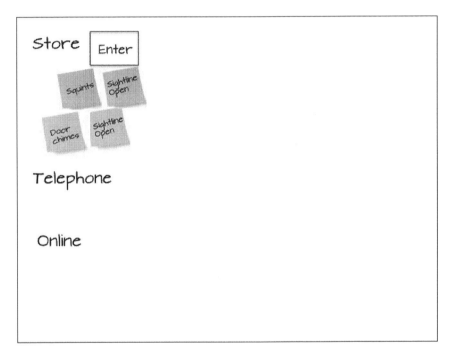

**Figure 4-2.** Customer Journey Map activity diagram, beginning

Identify the next interaction on the CJM and draw a square. For our example, that interaction is the customer being greeted by an employee, and the square is labeled "Greeting." Go through the same process as you did with "Enter," describing on the assigned colors of sticky notes the customer's experience now and as you want it to be.

A CJM can be as detailed or as high-level as you choose, based on how deeply you want to analyze—and improve—the live customer experience. However, even if you opt for detail, don't get mired down in minutiae. Rarely, if ever, is it necessary to map the experience for every product category or service you offer. You are mapping your customer's journey through the "forest," not their journey up to each tree within the forest.

For the specialty running store example, one of the additional types of interaction is "Browsing Product." Browsing is a "forest" activity—broad and big-picture. If we broke browsing down into subsections such as "browsing footwear," "browsing apparel," and "browsing accessories," we would be focusing on the trees and could miss the forest (a.k.a. big picture) entirely.

To flesh out the in-store experience for our example, we would add "Foot and Gait Analysis," "Footwear Fitting," and "Check-out" (the "finish" of the game board). For each of these steps along the path, the team follows the same descriptive process used with "Enter" and "Greeting." The end result of the Store path would look something like Figure 4-3.

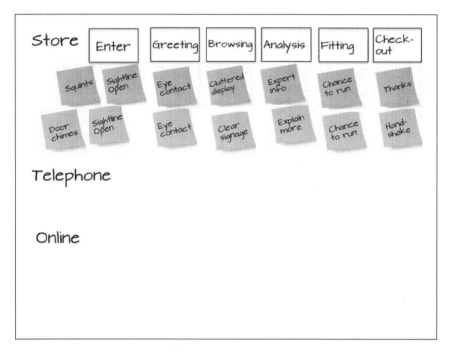

**Figure 4-3.** Customer Journey Map activity diagram, with one completed path

---

▓ **Note** Not all paths will contain the same number of steps. However, each path will have a start, at least one intermediate step, and a finish.

---

When all of your live customer experience paths on your CJM are complete, review them for commonalities. What shared experiences exist that you want to maintain or reinforce? Are there shared deficiencies between paths that demand immediate correction? Where can you invest your resources to produce the best possible outcomes and improve the live customer experience? Document all thoughts, ideas, solutions, and tasks, and sort them into one of four action lists with thirty-day, sixty-day, ninety-day, and undetermined deadlines. For example, if the running store customers are squinting as they enter the store because the lighting is inadequate, list "Change wattage of entry lighting; brighter bulbs" on the thirty-day action list. Notice the specificity of the action listed. That kind of detail empowers self-directed action among your team. Push yourself and your team to sort your ideas into the action lists with deadlines, because deadlines are the catalysts for completing any kind of task.

The undetermined action list should be the shortest of them all; ideally it is empty. A task without an assigned deadline has a high probability of lingering without completion. If you cannot determine a deadline for a task, you probably lack the proper information to make a determination in the first place. Therefore, shift your task to finding the information, and put a deadline on it.

When the thoughts, ideas, solutions, and tasks have been sorted into action lists, move on to assigning team members the responsibility of taking the lead in marshaling those tasks and getting them accomplished. Depending on the skill sets and personalities of your team members, the nature of your business culture, and your leadership style, team members could volunteer to lead, or you could directly assign them responsibilities as necessary.

# Align Employees to Customer Expectations

Understanding your customer and designing a live experience that is engaging and relevant is invaluable. However, the experience is of no value if your employees aren't aligned and committed to delivering on your customers' expectations. You may have heard the old expression, "You can lead a horse to water, but you cannot make him drink." Now that you've led your employees to the water (the experience your customer wants), this next design thinking tool will help you get your employees to drink (deliver the experience). The Code of Conduct exercise will help you lead your team *and* get them to drink.

## Code of Conduct

The title of this design thinking tool is a bit intimidating, and that's all right. Your ultimate outcome from the Code of Conduct exercise is a shared understanding among your team regarding what is required of them individually to deliver a meaningful live customer experience.

In the center of a whiteboard or flip chart, write the words "Pleasant" and "Meaningful." Ask each member of your team to call out what actions, behaviors, and beliefs they believe are necessary to make the live customer experience pleasant and meaningful. Write each thought and idea on your workspace in a mind map diagram. Group the thoughts and ideas around "Pleasant" and "Meaningful" as appropriate.

For the specialty running store example, contributions (Figure 4-4) could include "Make eye contact when you greet a customer," "Don't appear to be in a rush," "Shake the customer's hand at the end of the transaction, even if they haven't bought anything," and "Encourage the customer to be brutally honest about how the shoes feel."

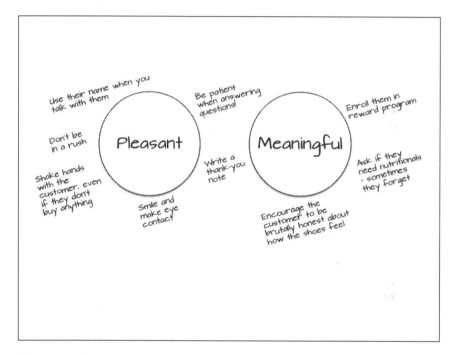

**Figure 4-4.** Code of Conduct activity diagram

Now quickly review each of the contributions and how they are grouped. Does everyone have the same understanding of each statement? Does everyone agree with how the statements are grouped? Is there anything missing? When your team is satisfied with the diagram, review each statement and ask why it is important to the live customer experience. Document their responses alongside the statement being addressed.

Once all statements have been reviewed and responded to, your diagram will resemble a work agreement that your team has co-created and to which they tacitly agreed. Your role at the end of the Code of Conduct exercise is to review the outcome with your team, noting each statement and the value they assigned to it. Remind them they now have a shared commitment to follow this code. Granted, it's a sneaky way to get employees aligned, but it works. The key is in the co-creation.

Enforcing the code of conduct and ensuring adherence to the commitment can be a challenge. Ideally, you'll have the type of business culture in which your employees can police themselves in a constructive way so that they keep each other focused and on task, without you needing to be directly involved. Unfortunately, there will be times when you have to step in and correct the behavior of either the code violator, the corrector, or both. It's a downside of being the boss.

Perhaps the best and most relatable example is parenting multiple children. I am a mother of four daughters, and they all know my and my husband's expectations for their behavior. They readily police themselves, and generally that works just fine. Occasionally, though, there are tattletale moments and I have to step in when self-policing is delivered in a nonconstructive way.

One means of ensuring enforcement of the code while minimizing your need to parent your employees is making the code part of your business's culture and conversation. Weave the content of your code of conduct into employee communications, add a review to the agenda of staff meetings, and consider posting the visualized code (Figure 4-4) in a break room or similar space as an ever-present reminder.

# Summary

Even though we live and work in a digitally dominated world, live experiences remain a significant and valuable interaction point between businesses and customers. They can make or break a customer's perception of your business and brand, and they are one of many areas that benefits greatly from the purposeful application of design thinking.

# Designing Digital Customer Experiences

## Creating Connections in the Digital Domain

The importance of live customer experiences is undeniable, and knowing that is incredibly valuable to your business and marketing planning. Also undeniable are the realities of our digital world and the evolving customer touch points that technology provides. A good digital experience isn't based just on functionality but on how your customer feels while interacting with it.

In the digital space, customer interaction is immediate and impatient. A customer can interact with your business and brand with intent ("I'm going to shop my favorite store online and buy some new clothes"), on a whim ("I wonder what time that movie is showing?"), or through happenstance (your digital presence is included in the results of an Internet search). A customer can interact with your business and brand online, via mobile technology, and through social media. Leveraging these possible means of interaction through technology requires a commitment to consistency in message, branding presentation, and quality across all digital platforms and devices.

# The Online Experience

Online experiences are now ubiquitous in business. Second only to developing a brand, creating a website is an immediate need for an entrepreneur or emerging business, and for good reason. To a customer, a website adds legitimacy and authenticity to a business; they expect to find a website that provides sufficient information, as well as opportunities to interact with the business in a way that meets their expectations. Often a website provides the customer's first experience with a business. As with live customer interactions, first impressions have impact.

Designing a relevant and meaningful customer experience in the digital realm involves more than just offering compelling graphic design and basic functionality. It requires a deep understanding of your customer that guides a thoughtful approach to information architecture, navigability, and usability. It also requires entering into the process knowing that until you've tested your website and are satisfied that it delivers what your customer wants, it is a prototype. Expect to have revisions even after you think you're done.

There are scores of digital agencies, freelancers, DIY software, and other resources to guide you through building a functional website. My purpose here is to give you a solid understanding of the process so that you are equipped well to work with, ask questions of, and challenge the assumptions of anyone with whom you work—including yourself—to develop your online presence.

## Information Architecture

Information architecture (often abbreviated IA) is simply fancy nomenclature for how your website's content is structured, shared, and found. The Information Architecture Institute defines IA formally as:

- The structural design of shared information environments.

- The art and science of organizing and labeling websites, intranets, online communities, and software to support usability and findability.

- An emerging community of practice focused on bringing principles of design and architecture to the digital landscape.[1]

---

[1] See http://www.iainstitute.org/en/about/our_mission.php.

As you discuss and design your website's IA, you need to consider first and foremost what your customer wants to accomplish by visiting your website. That is the foundation on which you build. The best way to illustrate the development of IA is through example. For simplicity, we'll use a service-based business as the case study.

Let's say you own a professional consulting firm and need to design its IA in preparation for developing a website. First, ask yourself why you need a website. In other words, what does your customer want to accomplish via your website? Your answers likely include finding your contact information, learning more about your services, learning more about your experience, and perhaps reading some case studies or testimonial statements from satisfied clients. Those answers identify the "big buckets," or main categories, of information.

IA designers represent this work visually through a tool called a wire frame, which looks a lot like an organization chart. The wire frame for our example would start out looking like Figure 5-1.

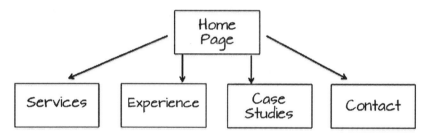

**Figure 5-1.** Wire frame example, tier 1

Now that you've defined your main information categories, you start on the next level of information. In the wire frame, this is the second layer in the chart (below the home page) and represents the information the customer wants to see if they click on one of your main categories. So in the consulting firm example, let's say the customer wants to learn more about the various services you offer. The second tier of information would include a list of services you provide, accompanied by brief descriptions. The wire frame would look like Figure 5-2.

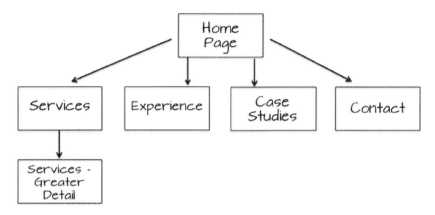

**Figure 5-2.** Wire frame example, tier 2

At this point, your IA may reach its conclusion for the services information, or it may need to expand. If you have only a few services and can sufficiently (and appealingly) describe them within a paragraph or two, you may not need another tier in the wire frame. If you need to provide greater detail, you might need another tier after all. If you need a third tier, the wire frame would look like Figure 5-3.

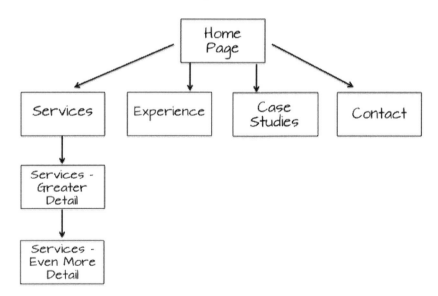

**Figure 5-3.** Wire frame example, tier 3

To flesh out the wire frame for your entire site, you would follow this process through each main information category to its natural end.

# Navigability

When you have a completed wire frame, the next step is to design the navigation of your website. Simply stated, you want to design how a customer moves through your site among the various pages of content.

Customers' web behavior is fickle, and because of that, great navigation walks a fine line between simplicity and annoyance. There's a general belief within digital marketing circles that a customer won't click through to another page within a website more than three times—less if they want to accomplish a specific task, such as contacting you. With each click, therefore, the content must be compelling and what they expect to see, or they may leave the site completely. Design your navigation to accommodate that fickleness.

Fortunately, there are a few widely accepted best practices for designing the navigability of your website. Leverage these! Don't let a web designer or other consultant try to convince you of something different. There are far too much data that support these best practices to ignore.

## Use a Top or Left-Side Orientation

First and foremost, embrace the fact that customers are habituated to look for the main navigation menu at the top or left side of your web page. Yes, it's predictable and somewhat boring, but it's easy and that's key. You'll notice that most of the popular templates, or themes, on Wordpress[2] (a type of web-based software for creating and hosting websites and blogs) have their main navigation in one of those areas. A few of the popular themes have images that dominate the top part of the page, with the navigation immediately below them. These themes defy the best practices I'm describing, so a word of caution: just because those themes are popular doesn't mean they are producing the best results.

---

▨ **Tip**　Keep your main navigation at the top of the page. It's the first place customers expect to see it.

---

## Use Descriptive Navigation

Second, make your main navigation descriptive. Although I've used "consulting services" in the case example, I encourage you to be more descriptive. If you consult on marketing, use "Marketing Consultation"

---

[2]See http://wordpress.org/.

in your main navigation. This level of specificity communicates directly to your customer and makes your site more visible to search engines. In fact, you may consider using highly targeted search terms or key words as your main navigation headings. Google offers a free tool called Keyword Planner that is easy to use.[3]

## Order Navigation Cues Carefully

Finally, consider the order of your main navigation. Items that appear first or last on any list are most effective, and navigation is no exception. Psychology studies on the "serial position effect" show that attention and retention are highest for things that appear at the beginning and at the end of lists. The middle gets lost in memory. Your navigation categories that are most important to your customers, and ultimately your business, should be listed first in your navigation. What about all of those websites you see with their "About Us" first in their navigation? Don't do that.

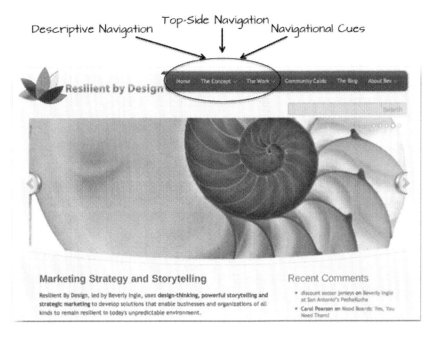

**Figure 5-4.** Navigation best practices

---

[3]See https://adwords.google.com/ko/KeywordPlanner/Home.

# Usability

With your navigation in place, the usability of your website comes to the forefront. The more usable the website, the easier for customers and the better their experience because it presents information in a clear and concise way and in locations that seem logical and lets them easily accomplish their goals.

---

■ **Tip** A website that is difficult or annoying will damage or destroy the digital experience and alienate customers.

---

Usability goes hand in hand with graphic design, so evaluating usability will run on a parallel path with the development of the website's graphics. The discipline of graphic design for the web is rife with best practices, technological protocols, and design accommodations that other media don't require. There are scores of other books devoted solely to web design and all its intricacies; this book is not one of them.

My intent in including usability as it relates to designing a digital experience is to highlight its fundamental importance. Usability is where the rubber meets the road, so to speak. All of your effort with IA and navigation is for nothing if customers can't easily use the resulting website.

## Keys to a Functional Website

As your graphic designer creates a functional website, there are best practices to ensure a usable product. Peter J. Meyers, the president of User Effect, compiled a twenty-five-point usability checklist[4] that is a great (though lengthy) resource. I consider five of them most critical to a website's effectiveness.

- Loading time for the site is reasonable. If your site takes too long to load, the customer will give up, and you've lost him or her.

- Good contrast between text and background and the font selection and size allow for easy readability. Customers don't want to squint or strain their eyes to read your information.

---

[4]See http://www.usereffect.com/topic/25-point-website-usability-checklist.

- Your logo is placed prominently, and your contact information is easily found.

- Use of buttons, links, and drop-down menus is reasonable. Thoughtfully guide your customer through your content; don't make them leap around to find the information they want.

- Content is concise, communicates clearly (i.e., can be skimmed and understood), and uses emphasis sparingly. The latter is particularly important. If too much of your content is emphasized through a boldface font or different text colors, or punctuated with too many exclamation points, how will your customer know what information is truly important?

The best way to determine the usability of your website is to test it. The best times to do this are early in the design process, when you can catch major flaws; when the design is complete but before the site is live; and any time you make major changes to the site. A good general approach to testing the usability of your site is to recruit five to ten individuals who best represent your primary customer demographically but who are not familiar with your website design. You might also consider participants who have varying levels of online experience. Generally, if you're testing early in the process, you need fewer participants to catch the big flaws. As the website gets more refined further in the process, you'll need more participants.

Don't let identifying and recruiting participants for testing overwhelm you. Much like recruiting participants for focus group research, start with the people you know in your professional and personal circles and expand from there. You probably won't have to look far to find amenable recruits. Once you have your testing cohort, it's time for evaluating your website.

Usability tests come in many different formats, and some agencies that specialize in digital design and development can make testing seem like an unwieldy beast to manage. It isn't. Usability tests can be simple and straightforward. At the end of the day, you want to know if your website works the way it should. Design your test to deliver that information.

## Design and Conduct an Effective Usability Test

To effectively design your usability test, outline what tasks you want the participant to do and the information you want to glean from that action. Then, draft directions and/or questions for the participants that will yield that information. For example, you might instruct them to locate and purchase a particular product, ask them where on the site they would find more information about the business's leadership team, or ask them to sign up for the newsletter.

Usability tests can be conducted in person by a moderator who guides the participants through the actions and observes the process. As with focus groups, you may want to record one or two participants, generally with the camera positioned over the participant's shoulder with their hands, the keyboard, and the computer screen captured in the frame. Usability tests can also be conducted remotely via a survey format, although this isn't as effective because you lose the opportunity for observation. In either case, at the end of the test, ask your participants to write a brief summary of their experiences, sharing any observations they have about functionality, navigation, and design.

Remember that at the beginning of this discussion, I pointed out that you need to consider your website as a prototype. Here's why: You will discover new things that require site changes.

After testing, review the data for its relevancy and determine what changes need to be made to remove any deficiencies. Certainly you want to create the best possible online experience for your customer, so don't cringe at the idea of revisions.

---

**Tip**    If the revisions to your site were extensive after the initial usability test, conduct another one. If the revisions were minor, then let your timeline and budget dictate whether you will do another round of testing.

---

# The Mobile Experience

Smart phones and mobile applications have evolved into critical touch points in the customer's digital experience. Because of that, businesses of all sizes and kinds are struggling to get ahead of the customer experience curve and find ways to drive brand engagement through mobile devices. Mobile technology puts Internet access, information, and social media in the hands of customers whenever they want it, wherever they are—and that's an immediacy you cannot afford to ignore.

Consider this scenario: Suzy Customer is in a coffee shop and wonders where she can find the designer handbag she's been coveting and finally decided to buy. She'll search the Internet for nearby stores so she can have it in her hands today. She finds your listing in her search results and clicks on your link. What will her experience with your business be through her mobile device?

Businesses that capitalize on the unique opportunities mobile devices present and purposefully design their digital customer experience to accommodate this technology can get ahead of their competitors. The key is to accept that mobile technology isn't simply a breeding ground for innovation. Rather, it is an important part of the business's overall customer experience ecosystem and an ever-evolving one at that. The following list suggests some of the best practices for mobile design[5]:

1. Put functionality first and visual design a distant second.

2. Performance is everything.

3. Keep it simple.

4. If a website will work, then skip the app.

5. Balance function, performance, and visual design for the best outcome. Too much of one thing isn't a good thing.

Designing for mobile technology often seems overwhelming. Ask for a mobile application and your designer/programmer will ask if it's for iPhone, Android, BlackBerry, iPad, or a netbook. (Each year there probably will be additional technology to add to that list!) Each device requires its own design to accommodate its operating platform and screen dimension. Imagine the costs of designing and programming for each type of device. Now imagine the costs of losing customers because you just didn't have the budget to develop an application for their type of device. Fortunately, there's been a shift in perspective among digital designers that is proving to be a huge benefit for businesses, especially those with limited resources for developing their digital presence.

# Responsive Design: An Alternative to Apps

As described in *Smashing Magazine,*

> *Responsive Web design is the approach that suggests that design and development should respond to the user's behavior and environment based on screen size, platform and orientation. The practice consists of a mix of flexible grids and layouts, images and an intelligent use of CSS media queries. As the user switches from their laptop to iPad, the website should automatically switch to accommodate for resolution, image size and scripting abilities. In other words, the website should have the technology to automatically*

---

[5]Adapted from http://www.adobe.com/inspire/2011/11/ten-best-practices-designing-mobile-websites.html.

*respond to the user's preferences. This would eliminate the need for a different design and development phase for each new gadget on the market.*[6]

---

▧ **Note**   Unless you have a very specific interaction you want your customer to experience or participate in, you probably don't need a mobile application.

---

For business professionals who aren't web designers, this description may sound like a foreign language. The most important part of it is, however, the last sentence, which loosely translated into business-speak means "budget-friendly." Responsive design largely eliminates the need for mobile apps in all but the most specialized customer interactions on mobile devices. Let's look at an example.

A local chapter of a nonprofit, membership-based social organization was concerned that it was missing opportunities to connect with and engage its current and potential customers (members) through digital media. Although it had invested significant financial resources in developing a content-rich web presence, the organization hadn't expanded its digital footprint to include mobile devices. The leadership felt that a mobile app would fill the gap, and they surveyed their membership to inquire about the type of mobile devices that were owned and used the most. The survey revealed three different types of devices for which applications would need to be designed. Unfortunately, the organization had limited resources to put toward development for even one app.

The organization's leadership worked with a web development consultancy, which helped them identify the types of interactions they wanted their members to be able to perform through mobile devices. These interactions mirrored those that could be performed on the group's website. An independent mobile app wouldn't be necessary to accomplish the organization's objective. Instead, the agency would restructure the group's website using responsive design techniques and mobile usability best practices. The end result was a digital experience in which the member could easily navigate and perform the key interactions in a visually appealing and efficient way—and consistent with the experience members would have online via the website—regardless of the type of mobile device they used. In simpler terms, a member could use his or her smart phone, netbook, or laptop and easily perform interactions in the same way successfully on each device.

---

[6]See http://coding.smashingmagazine.com/2011/01/12/guidelines-for-responsive-web-design/.

# The Social Media Experience

The third aspect of the digital customer experience trifecta is social media, and it plays an important role in creating an experience that supports a brand as well as delivering value to your customer in a way that resonates. Social media has also earned a reputation as a potential powder keg for businesses, but frankly, that's not entirely accurate. Social media in and of itself is a powerful communication tool. It offers a means to nurture connections with existing customers and connect your business with thousands of potential customers with which you might otherwise never have the opportunity to interact. The missteps of businesses in their use of social media is what has given the medium its stigma, and that can be assuaged by understanding its role and place in the customer experience landscape.

---

**Note**  Social media missteps, such as unauthorized Tweets or insensitive images on Facebook, can be a source of problems, but that's hardly a reason to avoid social media marketing efforts. When done right, they can enhance your brand, improve user experience, and give you an opportunity dialogue with customers.

---

Small businesses and entrepreneurs often see a great deal of success using social media as a means not only to communicate key information to customers but also help build a relationship with those customers and nurture loyalty. Clothing retailers provide great examples of this kind of interaction. Apricot Lane Boutiques, a franchised women's clothing retailer, engages customers on Facebook and Twitter with frequent posts about specific merchandise, sales, and events local to each boutique's market. The franchisees respond to customer questions and comments via social media, making use of the platform's two-way communication vehicles. Herein lies a critical point: this business understands that social media can—and should—be a way to speak *and* listen to their customers.

## Listening to Customers

Just as you can use social media to reach your customers and a wider audience of potential customers, so can your customers use social media to reach each other and that wider audience. Customers readily post their experiences—and their opinions thereof—in social media environments, most notably Facebook and Twitter. It's human nature to want to share one's experiences with others, especially when those experiences are emotionally charged. Social media gives them immediate outlets through which they can share, but that isn't always a good thing.

Customers might rave about the excellent service they received, describe a situation in which an employee went above and beyond to solve a problem, and encourage their friends and followers to support the business. In the glow of the feel-good moment, the satisfied customer can post a message from their smart phone on the spot. Definitely a desirable response!

Customers may also rage about an experience they perceive as less than ideal, whether it involved customer service, product performance, or operating policies. In this situation, the immediacy of social media can be a powder keg. In the heat of the moment, an angry customer can post a message without the benefit of having clearly thought through the comment or the potential effect of it.

In both situations, how the business responds will affect brand perception, customer loyalty, and the business's reputation.

---

▨ **Tip**   The way you respond to social media posts—what you say, when you say it, and how you say it—greatly affects the customer experience, for better or for worse.

---

## Reputation Management

Managing the customer experience in social media is frequently referred to as *reputation management*. That means monitoring social media platforms and engaging with customers appropriately, whether that involves answering questions, solving problems, or simply thanking customers for their support. It also means thoroughly understanding that there is no such thing as anonymity in digital media. Your activity in social media needs to be genuine and transparent as to its source. So whether you take on this responsibility, assign it to another team member, or contract with someone outside of your organization, reputation management is crucial to your business. The end goal is ensuring a positive digital experience for your customers.

Successful reputation management and positive customer experiences hinge on the timeliness, tenor, and content—in that order—of your response to a customer's comment, question, or complaint. For the most positive results, respond to any customer communication within an hour during normal business hours. If a customer praises you, thank them. If a customer has a question, answer it directly if you can be brief. If the answer requires a longer explanation, you can either ask the customer to email you or direct him or her to a specific page on your website where he or she can read the answer at length. Don't know the answer to the question? By all means, at least post a response along the lines of "Thank you for asking! Let me collect the accurate information, and I'll respond again soon."

---

▨ **Note**    The anonymity of digital media is a myth; your identity can be uncovered.

---

If a customer complains on social media, responding can be tricky and warrants greater care. The tenor and content of your response is crucial to resolving the situation to the customer's satisfaction and retaining your business's reputation and good will. Make a misstep, and your response could not only alienate that customer but also go viral and wreak havoc on your business's reputation. A customer complaint calls for a prompt, professional, succinct-but-not-curt, sincerely concerned response. Don't belabor the point, don't make excuses, and don't be defensive even if you feel the complaint is unjustified or vitriolic. Provide your contact information and ask the customer to contact you directly if they have any additional concerns or questions. If the complaint is specific to an employee, or if it will require additional action on your part to resolve, you'll want to move this conversation out of the public eye.

# Summary

Although the digital world in which we live and work is enduring, it is also evolving. What the digital landscape looks like today will be vastly different in a few short years. Technological advances result in new devices through which we can reach customers and digital environments in which we can interact with them. Regardless of how technology changes, the basis of our customer interaction stays the same. The quality of the customer's experience—not the vehicles through which it occurs—is what helps shape a business's success. As entrepreneurs and business owners, we need to keep our eyes on that prize.

Above all, remember to design the same positive experience with your customer in the digital space as you would if the customer was standing in front of you.

# Designing Services and Service Delivery

## Purposeful Customer Service

The playground of small businesses and entrepreneurs is not only product development but also services and their delivery. In fact, a service business is a common point of entry for entrepreneurship. On some level, almost everyone is qualified to start a service-based business, because everyone has some skill, knowledge, or experience for which others are willing to pay. Starting a service-based business is quite an egalitarian proposition; anyone with a decent work ethic and a desirable skill can sell a service; as opposed to product-based businesses, there is a reduced financial commitment because there is no physical inventory to purchase and maintain.

Differentiating your service business from the sea of others is equally as challenging as it would be with a product-based business. However, by applying a design thinking approach and using the discipline's tools, you can be purposeful where competitors may be haphazard.

▓ **Note** Design thinking can differentiate your offerings and help you stand out from the crowd.

# Services as Solutions

Just as a product must fulfill a customer need, a service must provide a solution to a customer's problem. For example, customers need a more fuel-efficient, high-capacity vehicle, so a U.S. car manufacturer produces a hybrid version of its best-selling SUV. The automaker's product fulfills a need. Furthermore, entrepreneurs and small-business owners need help getting everyday tasks done, so a software as a service (SaaS) company creates a web-based platform through which entrepreneurs and owners can contract with freelance assistants to accomplish those tasks. The SaaS company's service provides a solution.

Here is where the conversation about products and services can get esoteric. I have had many a colleague posit that a product can provide a solution, and a service can fulfill a customer need. Perhaps the hybrid SUV is the solution to a customer's transportation problem, and the SaaS company's platform is the product that fulfills the customer's need for an assistant. Do the semantics matter? Not all that much, but for our purposes of discussing the use of design thinking in developing services, we'll define services as solutions.

Successfully applying design thinking to a service business requires a solid understanding of the customer's problem for which the service is to be the solution. Chapter 2 covers the important role of research in the design thinking process. If you don't have a clear understanding of the problem for which the customer needs a solution, you simply cannot properly design a service to satisfy that problem. If you skipped Chapter 2, go back and read it now. If you've read it, remember that research helps eliminate assumptions, and design thinking research methods are affordable, accessible, and very user-friendly.

# The 5 Whys

With regard to service design, I highly recommend you use the 5 Whys as one of your design thinking tools (see Chapter 2 for a description). It is particularly important to understand the true root of the customer's problem to best design the service solution. Let's use a virtual assistant service as an example. At the surface, the belief is that entrepreneurs need help getting general business and personal tasks done. Why? Because they don't have time to do it all. The answer to "why?" may seem to be sufficient and a reasonable basis on which to design a service to solve the entrepreneur's problem. By digging deeper, however, we can design a service that delivers a more precise—and satisfactory—solution. Answers to additional why questions could reveal that ultimately, the entrepreneur doesn't have the expertise to handle specific tasks but won't or doesn't readily admit that to him- or herself.

---

▧ **Tip**   Embrace your inner toddler and enjoy asking "why?"

---

With a surface-level understanding of the problem, we may have designed the virtual assistant service to provide task fulfillment in a wide variety of areas performed by assistants with generalized experience. Instead, with a deeper level of understanding, we would design the service to offer assistance provided by more specialized experts to fulfill highly specific tasks in targeted areas of operations, such as finance or human resources.

# Making the Intangible Memorable

The one distinct feature of a service business that I encourage you to keep at the forefront of your mind and your awareness is this: services are intangible. Although services can be experienced and consumed, they cannot be physically touched, and their intangible nature produces some unique challenges with customers.

Services are at a great disadvantage as compared to products when it comes to forming lasting impressions among customers. Generally, services don't result in physical artifacts or tangible representations of the service that was provided. (Paperwork and forms—regardless of how classy their presentation folder is—do not count.) With product-based businesses, customers possess a physical artifact that they can identify with the business transaction, for example, an air-conditioning system, a car, a dress, or a watch. The artifact serves as a sort of memory device, prompting the customers to remember the business and their experiences interacting with it.

Intangible services are much like memories: they can be described in great detail, can be emotionally charged, and leave a lasting impression. Conversely, they can also be insignificant and transient. It's the quality and depth of meaning in what occurred that creates a lasting memory. It's also what gives a service its significance in the eyes and minds of customers.

To illustrate this dichotomy, I'll put the concept in personal terms: think of a vacation from which you brought home a souvenir, say, a seashell from the beach or a miniature Eiffel Tower from Paris. When you see that souvenir, do you recall the details of your vacation and all that you experienced? Now, think of a vacation from which you didn't bring home a souvenir. How often do you recall the memories of that trip? Can you recall those memories in rich detail, or are the memories a bit fuzzy?

---

▓ **Note**   Services lack the advantage of physical artifacts, which provide customers with visual cues to remember their interactions with a business.

---

A service business's lack of a physical artifact shouldn't be seen as a deficiency, but should be considered a ripe opportunity to engage design-thinking tools to ensure a service is delivered in such a meaningful way that it can be remembered in detail, over time, without the need of a visual prompt.

# Service Delivery Pathways

Service delivery seems inextricably linked to the customer experience, and from many viewpoints, it is. However, the focus of service delivery is efficiency and effectiveness—for your customer and your business—and it should be regarded as a distinct characteristic of your business and therefore planned and designed accordingly. The easiest way to view service delivery is to focus on the mechanisms through which your service is delivered. Let's go back to the virtual assistant service example to illustrate the difference.

An entrepreneur has decided to use your service to help her with book-keeping. How will you provide that service? In other words, through what paths can the customer engage your business, and at what points along those paths are there transactions through which you deliver your service?

The customer journey map (CJM; see Chapter 4) is an excellent design-thinking tool for mapping not only the customer journey, but also your service delivery process. If you've already completed a CJM for your business, bring the flip-chart pages out of your file drawer—or print out the digital photos you took of your completed map on the white board—and use them for reference. To incorporate your CJM into service design, you need to go a level deeper and add details of how your service is delivered to the customer.

There can be multiple starting points and service delivery pathways with any business. In our scenario, we'll compare and contrast two pathways. Both start online, and one remains online through the duration of the transaction, whereas the other goes offline to complete the service delivery in person.

Your entrepreneur customer goes online and reviews the content of your website (a pretty common occurrence in any business sector). Again, focusing on the mechanisms of service delivery and its roots in efficiency and effectiveness, how well does your website perform? Do the pages load quickly? Is the information clear and easy to understand? Is it clear to the customer what her next step needs to be to engage your company?

In our example, the entrepreneur reads on your website that to receive further information and a cost estimate, the next step is to submit an inquiry about services, describing what type of assistance she needs (see Figure 6-1). Is it clear via the copy and design how she is to submit that inquiry? Once she clicks on the link or button on the website, a fill-in-the-blank form pops up, with a request to provide as much information as possible. Are the form's fields defined in such a way that it guides her through providing the information, ensuring that you get the information you need?

## Virtual Assistant Service
*How can we help you?*

Thank you for contacting Virtual Assistant Service. We look forward to helping you. Please complete this form, providing as much detail as possible, and click the submit button. One of our team members will be in touch with you within 48 hours.

Name: _____ Company: _____

Type of Business: _____

Address: _____

Email: _____ Phone: _____

Please select the area(s) in which you need assistance:
☐ Office Administration ☐ Bookkeeping/Accounting ☐ Human Resources ☐ Sales Support

Please select the level of assistance you need:
☐ Entry-level (<3 years' experience) ☐ Mid-level (3-7 years' experience) ☐ Senior-level (+7 years' experience)

Must the assistant be available to work on-site at your office or business? ☐ Yes ☐ No

Please describe the activities with which you need assistance:



Please select how long you will need assistance:
☐ As-needed/On-call ☐ Short-term (<1 month) ☐ Long-term (1-3 months) ☐ Ongoing (>3 months)

☐ Submit

**Figure 6-1.** Inquiry form for service delivery

The form the customer receives—with defined fields—is designed to make service delivery efficient (Figure 6-1). By prompting the customer to provide detail up front and in a way that is helpful to you potentially will minimize the amount of communication needed before you can provide a cost estimate, thus making the delivery of service at this point more effective.

Once you have received the customer's form, identify how you will deliver the next level of service: the cost quote and the solution to the customer's problem. At this point the service delivery pathways can diverge into online-only and online/offline formats. As the service provider, you have a decision to make: how do your transactions need to happen? If research indicates that your customers prefer the efficiency of a completely online service experience, then that is the delivery pathway you design and provide. Alternatively, if research indicates that your customers are more likely to contract your services after meeting and conducting business in person, then you design your delivery pathway to start online and then move offline to close the deal. What if you don't have any research that indicates a preference? You can offer both and evaluate which means of service delivery performs better for you, or you can offer the service delivery that you prefer and monitor it closely to ensure you are able to meet your business goals.

In the virtual assistant services example, the steps along each pathway would have more differences than similarities (Figure 6-2). However you design service delivery, scrutinize the efficiency and effectiveness of each transaction point along the path. Not only do you want to ensure that the process is cost-effective for your business, you also want to minimize the risk of your customer abandoning the transaction altogether.

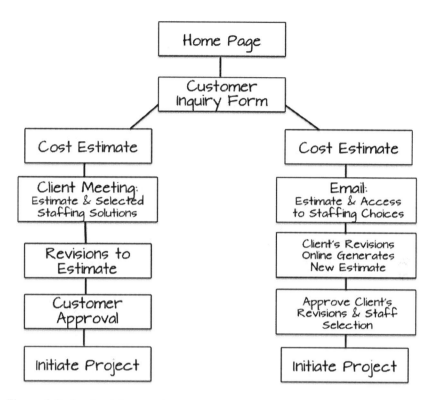

**Figure 6-2.** Service delivery pathways

# Risk of Abandonment

The phrase "abandon rate" has infiltrated many e-commerce conversations over the past five years, and it refers to how often an online customer starts but does not complete a shopping transaction. It's an alarming trend for businesses, and online retailers follow the data closely. Although it is well known that the "death rate" of customer transactions by abandonment is high for product-based businesses, I argue that the rates are likely higher among service-based businesses. Why? In my experience, the transaction points require a deeper level of engagement on the part of the customer before he or she has committed to the purchase. The form requires detail so that the next transaction is more effective. Providing that level of detail requires the customer to spend more time and thought early in the process and thus elevates the risk of abandonment.

Should we allow that risk to influence us to shorten the inquiry form and request less detail from the customer? There are arguments for yes and no. I am in the "no" camp; let me tell you why.

A service-based business by nature is more hands-on and generally requires more investment on the part of the business to complete a transaction (salespeople will tell you it's harder to sell a service than a product). As a business owner, I would opt to spend my investment on customers who are more engaged and by extension better prospects. A customer who has completed a more detailed form as part of an inquiry about my services demonstrates that deeper engagement.

Should we allow the risk of abandonment to influence us in how we design service delivery? Absolutely. I would be arrogant—and irresponsible—to suggest that service-based businesses don't need to be concerned about abandonment. The key here is to balance the business's need to invest in potential customers with the need to operate effectively and successfully. As one of my mentors would say, "Choose your battles."

In the war on abandonment, how do you identify which battles are worth fighting? I recommend using your CJM with the service delivery details and working with your team to identify points along the path at which customers may abandon the transaction. Any transaction point at which the customer has to make a decision is a potential abandonment point (see Figure 6-3).

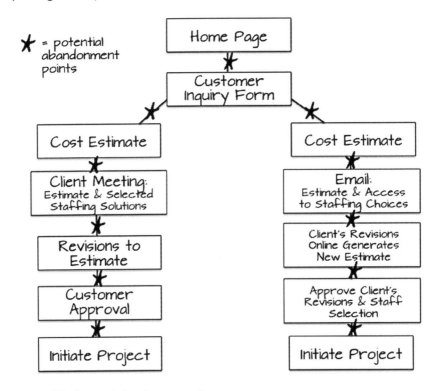

**Figure 6-3.** Potential abandonment points

Returning to the virtual assistant service example, abandonment can occur at many points, the first of which is when the customer reviews the website. As I noted earlier, if your pages load slowly, the information isn't clear, or there's no clear indication of what a potential customer should do to continue the transaction, the potential customer could bail. The detailed inquiry form could be an abandonment point. The cost estimate could also be an abandonment point. And so on.

Your challenge as a business owner or entrepreneur is to evaluate those potential abandonment points and prioritize them. For example, do you feel (and if you've done target market research, you likely know) that your prospective customer wants to be able to choose her own assistant from among the pool of resources you offer? Allow for that functionality. Is your prospective customer more likely to balk at the cost and potentially abandon the transaction at the cost estimate point? Consider redesigning the way you deliver that part of your service—presenting the estimate—via a meeting with the potential customer.

## Summary

Although service delivery and customer experience may seem like two sides of the same coin, they are in fact distinct aspects of business and demand individual attention. To best design the way your business delivers the service(s) it provides, acknowledge that the devil is in the details. Focus on the mechanics of how your services are delivered, with emphasis on efficiency and effectiveness for you and your customer. Well-delivered services produce great customer experiences.

# Designing Marketing

## More Than Meets the Eye

Proper, purposeful marketing is an integral part of a business's success. It is also one of the most volatile, subjective, and misunderstood areas of business operations. Although largely considered the fun part of business—with logos, tag lines, advertising, promotional items, letterhead, and so on—marketing done well is much more than meets the eye.

My professional background is in marketing. This subject is one of my passions, bailiwicks, and soapboxes. The discipline of marketing encompasses much more than the promotional activities such as advertising, public relations, and graphic design that immediately come to mind. Marketing in its true form also includes pricing strategy, product or service development, and product/service distribution. However, for the purposes of our discussion, when I refer to "marketing," I will be referring only to the promotional aspects of the discipline and how design thinking can enhance your efforts in that area.

▧ **Note** The terms *marketing*, *advertising*, and *branding* are often tossed around as though they are interchangeable, yet they are different disciplines.

Before you spend a penny on advertising, logo design, or any other marketing tactic, be sure you have a clearly articulated brand that you and your leadership team know inside and out. Without a doubt, the cornerstone of solid, successful marketing is creating a well-defined brand, and it should inform every marketing decision you make. To promote your business without this cornerstone in place is a waste of money.

Contrary to popular belief, defining your brand doesn't have to take forever or cost a fortune. By using design thinking tools, you can produce results quickly and efficiently. Once your brand is defined and in place, design thinking can help you create and execute marketing plans for products and services successfully.

# Rapid Branding

Know this: your business's brand is not a logo or a business card. Those are merely visual representations of your brand. Rather, your brand is your business's personality, the embodiment of what your company stands for and is known for. Your brand is what distinguishes you from your competition. When you market your brand, you are promoting that distinction, emphasizing your advantages to the customer, and positioning your brand as the solution to the customer's problem.

Accurately defining your brand can be accomplished in an afternoon with your senior leadership team or other important stakeholders using a design thinking activity called Microscoping. This activity helps you uncover your brand's DNA by exploring both the rational and emotional sides of your brand, drilling down to inviolate philosophies that reside at the core of your brand and form its essence.

# Defining the DNA

In the numerous times I have facilitated a Microscoping exercise, the first question from the team is invariably, "Are we defining the brand as it is now, or as it should be?" That one question immediately reveals that a brand is not in prime health. If the brand isn't the way it should be, there's no need to define it in its current state. Instead, define the brand as it *needs* to be.

The Microscoping exercise requires a white board (or flip charts), markers, and at least two hours of uninterrupted time with your leadership team. Prior to gathering your group, draw the chart shown in Figure 7-1, which will be populated during the exercise.

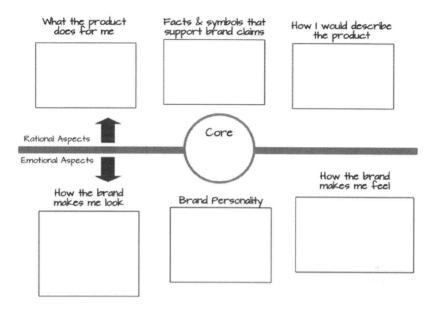

**Figure 7-1.** Microscoping brand DNA chart

The top half of the chart focuses on the rational aspects of the brand: what it does, how it could be described, and the facts and symbols that support the rational aspects. The bottom half focuses on the emotional aspects of the brand: how the brand makes the customer look, how it makes the customer feel, and its personality. At the center of the chart are three to five adjectives that describe the core essence of the brand, critical aspects that are never compromised.

Unlike other design thinking examples in previous chapters, this particular exercise requires a precise workflow for the best results. Starting with the top half of the chart, begin in the upper left quadrant and have your team define what your product or service does or provides in concrete, descriptive terms. To illustrate this process, we'll use a health care services start-up as an example. This start-up provides portable digital medical records, physician referrals, scheduling, and billing intermediation direct to consumers who join the program via a paid annual subscription.

Next, have your team define how the customer would describe the product. The health care start-up might be described as:

- a source of information,
- seems complicated but isn't,
- better access to physicians,

- worth the membership fee, and

- responsive to questions.

Now, consider the contents of the upper segments. What symbols and facts support the statements made? For example, symbols might include a USB drive, a medical bill, and a company representative on the phone. Facts might include, "patient access to all records," and "15 percent average reduction in patient out-of-pocket expenses," among others (see Figure 7-2).

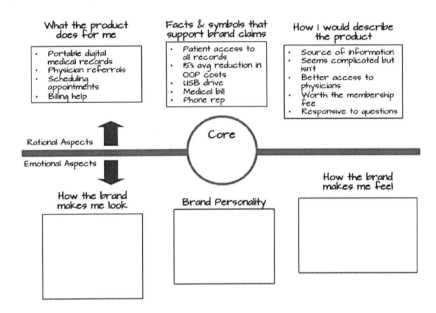

**Figure 7-2.** Microscoping brand DNA chart with rational aspects defined

Moving to the bottom half of the chart and beginning with the lower left box (Figure 7-2), describe how the customer thinks they look when they are associated with the brand. With our health care start-up example, descriptors of the customer could include technology-savvy, organized, sick, and needs help. Next, have your team describe how the customer feels when they are associated with the brand, and fill in the lower right segment. For our example, descriptors might include empowered, safe, thankful, informed, and helpless. Considering the content of the bottom segments, have your team describe the personality of the brand. Our health care start-up's brand personality might be described as helpful, friendly, knowledgeable, and accessible.

With all of the quadrants complete (Figure 7-3), and the facts, symbols, and personality described, the team moves to the center of the chart, where the core of the brand is defined. The discussion must focus on the aspects of the brand that the business must never abandon to keep itself distinct from its competition, relevant to its customer, and viable to its stakeholders.

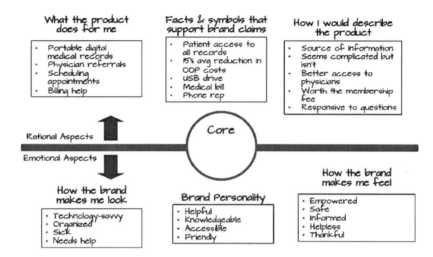

**Figure 7-3.** Microscoping brand DNA chart with emotional aspects added

At this point in the Microscoping activity, the conversation gets more difficult. You and your team must winnow the information in the boxes down into a core that contains an immune, bite-size conviction. This is no easy process. Teams inevitably lean toward defining the core too expansively. However, it is important to embrace the reality that your brand cannot be all things to all people. As a former colleague of mine used to say, you have to stick a stake in the ground and stand by it. The core of your brand is your stake in the ground.

---

■ **Tip**   If you're using flip charts for the Microscoping exercise, consider using a pencil when defining the core. You'll probably have revisions as the team discusses the core aspects. Once the team has agreed on the final content, go back and add that in with a marker. You'll have a better-looking final document.

---

To best define the brand's core, use key words from the content in the graph. For longer statements and phrases, use words that succinctly capture their essence. Those key words for our health care example could be *helpful, knowledgeable, data, access, technology, referrals, empowered,* and *safe.* However, eight words are too many. It becomes too large of a conviction to be able to support sustainably. The challenge is to narrow that list to no more than five, so the team ultimately asks themselves the hard question, "What is absolutely mandatory for our brand's success?" The answers form your brand's DNA.

Now that you have your brand's DNA defined, use it as your touchstone for all communications—internal and external—as well as product or service development. With our health care example, let's say we whittled the list down to these three: *access, helpful,* and *safe* (Figure 7-4). In advertising, staff newsletters, web content, and so on, the key messages the company conveys would always support at least one of the key words. Furthermore, as the product development team fleshes out the offerings to the company's members, they would measure their efforts against those key words. For example, they might ask themselves in the process, "Is this product designed to reinforce our brand's core?"

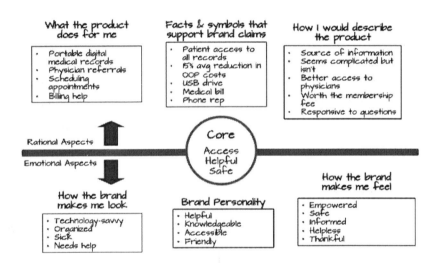

**Figure 7-4.** Microscoping brand DNA chart completed

# A Family of Brands

Just because you operate a small business or are an entrepreneur with a start-up does not mean that you won't need to design and manage multiple brands. It is important to use the Microscoping exercise for each brand in your company's portfolio. They may have some commonalities, but I guarantee they will have their distinctions, and those need to be defined and articulated. Don't take shortcuts and assume that because you defined your company's brand DNA that the new product you added or the competitor you acquired will share it.

To best illustrate this, let's look an example of a much larger company that operates on a global scale: Procter & Gamble. All companies have a starting point, and Procter & Gamble (P&G) is no exception. It was once a small(ish) company like yours. Today, though, the company's brand portfolio is large and diverse with brands ranging from Tide and Downy to Secret and Tampax. A review of statements that dominate P&G's website reveals that its corporate brand DNA focuses on value, innovation, and sustainability.[1] As a consumer, think about P&G's brand DNA in relation to Tampax. At Tampax's core is the brand about value, innovation, and sustainability? No. Tampax's marketing and branding statements emphasize confidence and freedom. However, Tampax does share innovation as a characteristic of its brand DNA, thus keeping the product relevantly tied to its parent company. Tide also embraces innovation as part of its brand DNA, keeping it tied to P&G. In fact, you'll see the innovation thread running through all P&G product brands.

When a company has a portfolio of more than one brand, you can look at it as a family of brands. As with the P&G example, the parent company shares some of its DNA with its offspring—brands—just as the parents of a family share genetic material with their children. Obviously not all children in a family are identical replicas of the parents; each sibling is different, but they share some commonalities that indicate they are part of the same family and of the same parents. The same applies to a parent company such as P&G. Its brands share some commonalities, but each brand is different in its own right.

As your company expands, keep this family perspective in mind. You want each brand to be resonant of the parent brand's DNA, but you need to define them on their own terms so they can grow, strengthen, and succeed independently of the parent company.

# Designing a Marketing Plan

With your brand DNA defined and articulated for the entire world (or at least your world) to see, you can confidently design a marketing plan that will appropriately support your brand. Your brand DNA is your touchstone, and your marketing plan is your roadmap. Its entire purpose is to get you from point A (where your business and brand is now) to point B (where you want it to go/what you want to achieve).

---

[1] See http://www.pg.com/en_US/index.shtml.

Imagine heading off on a road trip with a destination in mind but only a general sense of how to get there and nothing to guide you. How many times might you take a wrong turn, have to backtrack, end up taking a much longer and circuitous route, and arrive stressed and late to your destination? Contrast that experience with a road trip for which you have directions and landmarks, and an accurate determination of the length of your trip so that you arrive at your destination energized and ready to go?

I have always followed a formulaic approach to designing a marketing plan. It keeps me on task and prevents overlooking key factors relevant to the plan. However, the resulting document can vary in length depending on the scope of the marketing effort and the level of detail put into the plan. Before you start designing a plan, consider your audience: for whom is this plan intended? A leadership team well versed in your brand's DNA, your target market, your marketing goal, your budget, and your key performance indicators may need less detail than a collaborative team comprised of leaders from different departments, vendors, or others not involved in your company's daily operations. Let your audience be your guide when determining the level of detail to include in the plan. A marketing plan template is provided in the resources section of this book, Appendix D, for your use.

# The Business Case

The opening section of a well-designed marketing plan is pretty cut and dried: what is the business case for what you want to accomplish? Generally a paragraph or two, this section is a brief summary of the justification of your marketing plan. Use data to support your case and answer the question, "Why do we need to market this?"—particularly if you are marketing a specific product or service. Returning to our health care start-up example, the business case could center on reducing the time and expense required to navigate the health care system.

# Strategic Overview

Follow your business case with a description of your business, product, or service and why it effectively satisfies the business case. This section is also typically a paragraph or two in length. For our example, the health care start-up's services are designed to intermediate on behalf of patients and give them access to resources to more easily navigate the health care system.

# Marketing Objectives

Next, outline your marketing objectives. You can describe these or simply list them as bullet points. These objectives should illustrate the "big picture" you want to accomplish with this marketing plan. In the case of our example, the marketing objectives could be to:

- increase awareness of the start-up's services among the target markets,

- position the start-up as the solution to the customer's frustrations, and

- add 200 new members.

Stating marketing objectives—at the very least, one of them—in terms that can be measured is important, as you'll discover further into this chapter.

# Communications Objectives

These objectives are more granular in detail than the marketing objectives. They focus on the tactical approach to communications that the company will take to satisfy the marketing objectives. You can describe these objectives or list them as bullet points. Our start-up example's communications objectives could include planning and launching a customer-directed, highly targeted, direct-response campaign and implementing a public and media relations effort to increase awareness of their services.

# Target Audiences

Your business will probably have more than one target audience. Remember, though, that you want the best return on your marketing investment, so you want to keep your marketing plan focused on the one or two audiences that will provide you with the greatest opportunity for return. The research you've conducted (see Chapter 2) will guide you in describing your primary—and perhaps your secondary—target audience. In this section, you provide a narrative description of the target audience, as well as any relevant demographic data. For our health care start-up, the primary target audience may be married women, ages twenty-five to fifty, employed outside of the home, with children under the age of eighteen, who have visited a physician, medical clinic, or hospital at least three times within the past twelve months.

# Marketing Strategies

In this section, the plan begins to show some greater detail with more specification as to how the team will go about accomplishing the marketing objectives. The marketing strategies you outline should be broad strokes of activity, such as designing the communications with a consistent theme that also drives customer inquiries to a campaign-specific web address through which customers can access more detail and the company can capture customer data. Notice that the details of what that theme entails or the design of the communication devices are not included at this point. To provide that level of detail at this early stage of planning would be premature.

# Key and Supporting Messages

This section can be included in the marketing plan, or it can be omitted depending on the process you and/or your team went through in designing the plan. If, during the plan design phase, you hit on the key customer message—and any supporting messages—to meet the plan's objectives, this section is where you would describe it and any specific word choices that should be used in customer-directed communication. For example, with the health care start-up, that key message could be about providing confidential and helpful support to aid members in accessing needed health care resources.

# Tactical Plan

Now it's time to outline the nitty-gritty details of your marketing plan. Whereas the previous sections of your plan serve as your overarching guide, this section gets granular in its detail. In your tactical plan, you articulate what you'll do to follow your strategies and use your key messages to accomplish your objectives. Open your tactical plan by addressing all of the planned resources you'll use to fulfill the plan's objectives: advertising and promotional vehicles, community outreach activities, public and media relations efforts, and so on.

I encourage you to include as much detail as possible. With our health care start-up example, we might list highly targeted direct mail, a search engine marketing campaign, and social media advertising as three vehicles through which the start-up will promote its services to its target audience. Although that list provides a nice overview to your promotional activities, make an effort to add specifics. For example, with regard to the direct mail tactic, the company might include detail on the format of the direct mail piece itself (brochure, postcard, etc.), the source of the mailing list (Experian, health care provider partners, etc.), the mailing list parameters (the target audience demographics plus any behavioral qualifiers such as "active in outdoor sports" or "expecting a new child within the next six months"), and the frequency planned for the mailing (three separate pieces mailed within eight weeks). Do this for each of the resources you listed as tactics.

To accompany the detailed outline of resources to be used, create a timeline to delineate what happens and when. (I prefer to keep things simple and use a spreadsheet as a calendar, with each field representing one week.) Continuing with the start-up's direct mail example, we would identify the dates on which we want the pieces to be sent and add the relevant dates for the other resources.

# Measurement

The final section of your marketing plan should address how you will measure your efforts in all areas to determine their level of success. Nine times out of ten, our immediate response to the question, "What does success look like?" is "More _____," with the blank filled in by "sales," "customers," "accounts," or "business." We all want more, but we need to be specific in our marketing plan. I am a firm believer that marketing efforts *alone* cannot be responsible for generating new business. There are too many other factors out of the purview of marketing that influence a customer's buying decision. Marketing can and should be accountable for increasing awareness, influencing brand perception, and activating customer inquiries.

---

**Tip** Plan to measure all marketing efforts. How else will you know what's working and what isn't?

---

When you have multiple tactics supporting your marketing plan, as with our start-up example, you need to decide if you want to measure the performance of the marketing campaign as a whole or measure each tactic individually. For our start-up, measuring on the whole is as easy as tallying the number of new members acquired during the campaign and within thirty days after. If you want more detailed analysis and measurement, each of your resources needs to be measured in terms of key performance indicators (KPIs) that are relevant and realistic for that resource.

To illustrate, let's put this in terms of our start-up's direct mail tactic. As stated in the marketing objectives, the company wanted to enroll 200 new members. Can direct mail be solely responsible for producing those new members? No, that would be an unrealistic KPI. The direct mail might make a compelling case, but chances are good that only a small portion of recipients will become new members based on that one communication tactic. Probably more new members will originate through the other planned communication vehicles, as well as through inevitable phone inquiries for more information. (Never overlook the power of a personal conversation between a potential customer and one of your team members!)

Can direct mail be expected to drive customer inquiries, thus potentially generating new members? Absolutely, and that's a reasonable KPI for that tactic. Now that the KPI for direct mail is established, how do you determine the quantity of inquiries the direct mail should generate? Fortunately, there are "industry standards" and best-practices expectations you can use as guidelines. For direct mail, the expected response rate, which is what yields your quantity of inquiries, is between 3 percent and 5 percent of the total number of pieces mailed. That translates into 30 to 50 responses per 1,000 pieces mailed. The more targeted your mailing list, the more likely the response rate will be higher.

As you assign KPIs to your tactics, make note of the expected performance. I often include this information on the tactical timeline/calendar, updating it weekly, so I can visualize progress during the duration of the marketing campaign.

## The Doctor Is In

Throughout this book, I've emphasized the importance of understanding your customers, their wants, and their needs so that you can design your business and its products or services as the solutions. You need that same understanding for successful branding and marketing. You must understand your primary customer to define your brand in terms that they will find resonant, which will lead to affinity and preference.

At some point in your business's life cycle, you'll encounter an inevitable ebb in your success, and there could be any number of causes for this. Among all of the introspection and analysis you will deploy during slow times, be sure to include a health check-up for your brand. A brand that is healthy, that is, relevant, recognized, and profitable, is one of the many business Sherpas that carry your business along the path to success. A brand that is unhealthy can be your undoing even when all else is going well.

Determining your brand's health status requires some serious introspection, a willingness to inquire of and listen to others, and an open mind receptive to what is shared. The best way to undergo a brand health check-up is with an activity called The Doctor Is In. This activity requires you and your team to answer some hard-hitting questions in descriptive detail to best ascertain what "ails" your brand. The doctor asks questions to uncover the symptoms of the ailment. If the first round of answers don't provide sufficient detail, the doctor probes deeper with follow-up questions such as, "Then what happens?," "What changes did you see?," and "Why or why not?" The following list consists of core questions for the doctor to pose to yourself and your team. It was born from my professional perspective and evaluation process, and feel free to modify it as you see best for your unique business. I strongly recommend you use a moderator to serve as the doctor. For fun, I always draw a graphic that resembles Lucy's "psychiatric help" stand from the Peanuts comic strip and put the answers to the questions in the center (Figure 7-5).

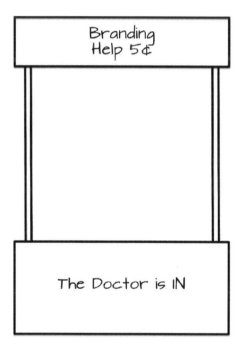

**Figure 7-5.** Graphic for The Doctor Is In activity

The Doctor Is In Questionnaire

1. How is your business changing? Are you merging, changing your product or service offerings, or revising your strategic plan? Has customer attrition been higher than normal?

2. How is your market changing? Are there changes that affect your customers' behavior? Are you facing new or increased competition?

3. Is your industry becoming commoditized?

4. Is your core customer base changing? Do you have different customers now than you did five years ago?

5. If you ask ten people closely associated with your business, "What is our mission?" will you get ten different answers? Or worse, blank stares?

6. Do your communications (brochures, manuals, advertisements, promotional pieces) present consistent messaging? Or do they look like they could be from different companies?

7. Do you lack comprehensive brand and messaging guidelines that are consistently used by everyone internally and externally who are creating communications materials?

8. Can you tell your business's story in three minutes or less?

Notice that the first and second questions focus on *how* change is happening, not *if* it is. Change always takes place; it's the pace of it that changes. If your business or market is changing more rapidly than you can keep pace, you have some fundamental operations issues to address; put your brand on the back burner until that is resolved.

If the third and fourth questions give you cause to stop and think, you may not be paying close enough attention to the change that surrounds you, and your brand is suffering for it. You might consider reviewing Chapter 3 and adjusting your business strategy as needed to accommodate the shifts in your industry and customer base.

Questions five through eight are all communications-based and directly related to your brand's health on a micro level. Even if you have pressing macro issues that have been revealed with the first four questions, you can work immediately on a short-term remedy for your brand in this area.

The essence of marketing is the ability to tell a compelling story, and telling it in a way that is relevant to customers and your own team. As business owners and entrepreneurs, we often overlook the importance of telling our story internally. We often think that because our team is immersed in our business daily, they know the story and understand its meaning. That isn't always the case. If others closely associated with your business—employees, leadership, and key vendors—can't share a synopsis of your story, you need to tell it to your internal audiences more frequently and more comprehensively.

If your communications materials aren't presenting a consistent message and image, then not only are they not sufficiently supporting the story you and your team are telling, they are also not telling an accurate story in the absence of the narrators. Communications materials absolutely must tell your story, emphasizing strengths, differentiators and compelling facts, on their own. They also must present a visual image consistent with the attributes of your brand. This applies to materials presented to customers as well as internal documents.

An easy (and, sadly, prevalent) example to point out is a business's email signature, because email is used both externally and internally. How many times have you seen variations of an email signature sent from a company-based email address? One may have the full-color logo and another with none. One sender may include the business's website address and no social media links, and another sender may leave off the website but still include the social media links. Confusing, isn't it?

Last, as the head honcho of your business, you must be able to tell your story to anyone of any background succinctly and effectively. Yes, I'm referring to the fabled and often-maligned *elevator pitch*. Your short story, so to speak, will be a necessity for the life span of your business, and if you can't nail it, you certainly can't expect others to do so. Practice if you need to. Craft variations on a theme so you're prepared for any type of listener, from your barber to the angel investor you lucked upon in the conference center hallway.

## Summary

Marketing provides the opportunity to tell your brand story in a purposeful way to the audiences who will most likely find the greatest meaning and relevance within it. Just as with other aspects of your business, design thinking provides valuable perspective and guidance to help you achieve the best outcomes. From discovering and defining your brand's DNA through Microscoping to evaluating your brand's health with The Doctor Is In, design thinking tools can put you and your team in the much-desired position of market leader.

# Designing for Change

## Don't Get Caught Off-Guard

Change is inevitable. Even if you dig in your heels and fight it every step of the way, change still happens. It can seem interminably slow, or faster than the speed of light. The sheer number of clichés and colloquialisms to describe change is an indication of its inevitability. We've grasped at grammatical straws to come to terms with the flow of change. It's important to understand that change doesn't have to happen to you. I encourage you to use design thinking tools to make change happen for you and for your business's success.

## Going Beyond Your Gut

Many of us have a strong gut instinct, and most of us tend to follow it. I think it's one of the more distinctive qualities of entrepreneurs and small business owners—knowing that you have a great idea and being willing to take a leap of faith to make a business out of it. Successful entrepreneurs and business owners back up their gut instincts with smart and diligent business planning.

Changes in market conditions, economies, industries, and niches don't have to catch you unaware and unprepared. Regardless of the scope of change, you can anticipate it, stay attuned to its subtleties, and take purposeful steps toward using it to your benefit.

---

▧ **Tip**　If it seems as though nothing is changing, then you aren't looking closely enough.

---

Up to this point, the opportunities to apply design thinking principles to the development of products, services, experiences, marketing, and physical spaces have been pretty clear. Needs and challenges could be identified and articulated, and uncovering potential solutions could be approached methodically. Facing change and designing for it is quite a different scenario. Change can be rife with ambiguity, making it harder to pinpoint how you can intervene in its emergence and purposefully design your response to it. All the more reason to employ design thinking.

# Facing Change Head-On

You've heard the bit about not seeing the forest for the trees. There's legitimacy in that idiom, as you have probably experienced. All too often, as we are immersed in our own daily ins and outs of operating our businesses, we focus only on what is within our immediate view, the "trees:" next week's payroll, next season's futures, last month's sales figures, next year's goals. Meanwhile, we have little idea what might be happening in the forest because we aren't looking. The "forest"—the bigger economic picture—may be undergoing radical change that could yield either great opportunity or portend disaster.

How do you see the forest and not just the trees, then? Use the Forest and Trees design thinking activity.

At its root, the Forest and Trees activity is a sorting tool, albeit on a big-picture scale. Use it to distinguish between issues with shorter-term, more intimate ramifications and those issues that have the potential to have a more profound effect not only on your business, but also on the economic environment in which you operate.

Gather your leadership team for this activity, which can typically be completed in less than two hours. Using two flip charts, or a large white board divided in half, label the left side "Trees" and the right side "Forest" (Figure 8-1). Provide your team with stacks of sticky notes and ask them to list all of the issues that consume the majority of their time, one per sticky note. This should not be a list of what the participants do each day, but a list of the challenges they face on a regular basis and that require their time and attention. The information contributed can vary widely, encompassing everything from human resources and team management to product development and operations. Assemble the sticky notes into themes—all of the operations issues together, and so on—and arrange them under the Trees heading.

# Trees | Forest

**Figure 8-1.** Forest and trees chart, in progress

Now it's time to view your trees in the context of the forest. Working through one theme at a time, have your team evaluate each issue for its relevance to the larger environment. For example, let's say a financial planning firm has identified trees and sorted them into the following themes: human resources, sales, and industry regulations. As the team works through the human resources theme, they are particularly vocal on the issue of talent acquisition and the increasingly difficult process of identifying and attracting the knowledgeable and skilled professionals they need to grow the business. The question to ask: "Is talent acquisition an issue beyond our business?"

To determine the answer, the team needs to have some working knowledge of the greater economic environment and developments in their specific industry. Is the topic of talent acquisition in relevant news sources? Is it a topic of conversation and industry-related events? Within the past year, have they found themselves in a bidding war for talent with a competitor outside their market? Positive responses to these types of questions likely indicate that the issue is affecting the forest, so a sticky note with *talent acquisition* would then be posted to the Forest side of the board.

Keep working through each theme on the Trees side until they have all been evaluated and duplicated for the Forest side of your board as needed. Once you are finished with the trees, it's time to expand your perspective and evaluate the forest by asking your team, "What issues are you seeing or hearing about that haven't affected us yet?" Again, working knowledge of the bigger economic environment and your industry is necessary for effectiveness. As you did with the trees section, list each forest issue on sticky notes, one per note, and sort them by theme on the Forest side of your board (Figure 8-2).

**Figure 8-2.** Forest and trees chart, completed

Once your forest issues have been identified, it's time to evaluate them in the context of the trees. Consider the financial planning firm example. Perhaps the team listed recently passed legislation in a state in which the firm does not operate. They would need to answer the question, "What is the likelihood that similar legislation could pass in our state, and how would it affect our business?" If the team determines that the likelihood is high, the next step is to write the issue on another sticky note and post it on the dividing line between forest and trees.

At the conclusion of the Forest and Trees activity, you and your team will have a map of sorts that will help you visualize the larger "forest" issues, that is, impending change, that could have ramifications for your business, which will help you in taking the next steps toward designing for that change.

# The Need for Speed

The Forest and Trees activity can be somewhat intense because you and your team are immersed in a lot of deep, evaluative thought. You've seen the forest and the changes approaching on the horizon. Seeing isn't enough, though. Your team needs to be able to respond to that approaching change. To do that, and to enjoy an exercise that provides some mental and emotional balance to the intensity of Forest and Trees, follow with a faster-paced design thinking exercise called 3-12-3.

The 3-12-3 exercise is a three-part activity in which strict timekeeping is the main rule, and the numbers refer to the amount of time allotted for each part: three minutes for generating ideas, twelve minutes for combining those ideas into rough concepts, and three minutes again for presenting the concepts to a group. The process is all brainstorming, but the approach to it is focused and fast, forcing the participants to generate ideas quickly without a lot of overthinking.

To start the activity, identify the problem, opportunity, or issue for which you need some potential solutions and state it in no more than two words. Although you could identify the issue with a descriptive sentence or phrase, resist this temptation. Keeping it limited to just two words supports the brevity of the activity. Referring back to our financial planning firm example, let's say that the issue at hand is "talent acquisition." On a white board or flip chart, write "Talent Acquisition" as the heading. If you have more than five team members participating in this exercise, divide them into equal-size groups, but don't have more than three groups total.

Next, give each of your participants a marker and a stack of sticky notes, along with the direction to generate as many ideas as possible in three minutes for how they and the company might be able to solve the issue of talent acquisition. Once those three minutes are up, be firm about stopping the brainstorming. (Remember, speed is important in this activity!) For our financial planning firm example, some of those ideas could include developing a proprietary training program, partnering with a local college or university to ensure its curriculum aligns with current industry needs, or hiring a full-time recruiter in the company's human resources office.

Following the three-minute brainstorming, give participants twelve minutes to organize their ideas and group them into themes. Our financial planning firm example may group its ideas into themes like education, staffing needs, or internal training (Figure 8-3). As participants sort their ideas into themes, they can sketch, draw, or otherwise visualize their ideas to better communicate the concepts, with the goal of being able to communicate them clearly to the larger group in the last part of this exercise.

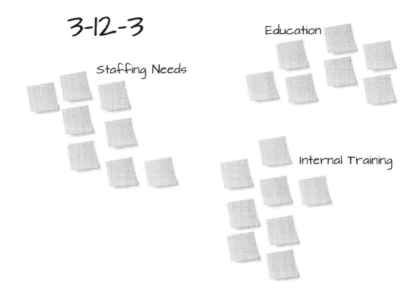

**Figure 8-3.** 3-12-3 activity chart

Furthermore, as they work through the sorting process, they will discover how the ideas may be interrelated and may see additional opportunities. If the sorting portion of the 3-12-3 exercise spurs new ideas, have your participants capture those ideas but keep them separate for later consideration. If you see your participants starting to brainstorm during this twelve-minute period, redirect them back to sorting the ideas that have already been generated.

The last three-minute section of the exercise can take one of two paths. If your group of participants was large enough to be divided into separate smaller groups, then the smaller groups each have three minutes to report on their ideas and how their thought process worked—quickly and succinctly! Again, each group has only three minutes for this part. If your team is smaller and they all worked together as one unit, these three minutes can be spent synthesizing the themes or summarizing the conclusions drawn during the sorting segment of the activity.

To conclude the 3-12-3 activity, collectively reflect and discuss what ideas were shared, but don't be satisfied with just reflection. Take the opportunity to make the effort that went into the activity actionable. Save the sticky notes from 3-12-3 and use them in the next design thinking exercise.

# The Matrix Holds the Answers

If you have gone through the previous two design thinking activities, you and your team have seen the approaching changes (a.k.a. the forest) and generated ideas of how to best respond. To make your efforts actionable, you need to evaluate your concepts and select those in which the company should invest more time and resources. The Impact and Effort Matrix is an excellent design thinking tool for helping teams choose among its options.

The Impact and Effort Matrix is a decision-making exercise in which possible actions are evaluated and mapped based on two qualities: the effort required to implement the action, and the action's potential effect on the group's issue, opportunity, or challenge. Some actions may be inexpensive and easy to implement but may make very little impact. Others may be expensive but have a sizable long-term payoff that justifies the expense. Categorizing actions in this manner helps decisions get made, because participants must balance and evaluate potential actions reasonably before committing to them.

On a white board or large flip chart, draw a large square. Label the left line of the large square "Impact," and label the bottom line "Effort." Place a minus sign at the intersection of these two lines. At the opposite end of each line, place a plus sign (Figure 8-4).

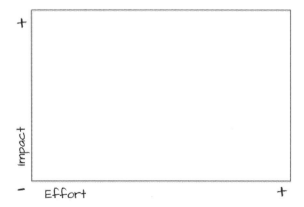

**Figure 8-4.** Impact and Effort Matrix chart, in progress

Now divide the large square into four smaller squares. In the upper left quadrant, draw a happy face. In the lower right square, draw a sad face. In the upper right and lower left quadrants, draw questioning faces. Now, the matrix is ready to accommodate mapping the team's ideas (Figure 8-5).

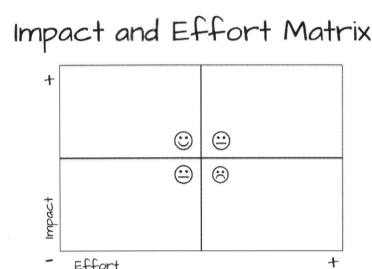

**Figure 8-5.** Impact and Effort Matrix chart, ready for input

To open the exercise, ask the group a question, which can be as simple as "What do we need to reach our goal?" For the financial planning firm and its challenge with talent acquisition, the question might be "How do we find the talent we need?" Ask the group to generate ideas individually on sticky notes, and add those to the notes you saved from the 3-12-3 activity, discarding any duplicates.

Ask the group to present their ideas and place them within the Impact and Effort Matrix according to their perception of the amount of effort required to implement the ideas and the degree of impact those ideas are likely to have (Figure 8-6).

# Impact and Effort Matrix

How do we find the talent we need?

**Figure 8-6.** Impact and Effort Matrix chart, complete

As participants place their ideas into the matrix, they may—and should—openly discuss the position of the ideas. The group might strengthen an idea and therefore move it up in impact or down in effort. An idea might also be degraded and moved up in effort or down in impact. Ultimately, the collective wisdom, experience, and opinion of the group will direct the idea to its proper position within the matrix. In this respect, the high-impact/low-effort square will house the ideas to which the group is most committed, and those ideas should be considered the most actionable.

---

**Note** Collaboration and cooperation is critical in the matrix.

---

Returning to our financial planning firm and its talent acquisition example, ideas that could reside in the high-impact/low-effort square could include such things as an internal training program, a more rigorous evaluation of skills during the interviewing process, and developing a list of educational institutions whose curricula align best with the firm's skill set needs.

## Summary

As entrepreneurs, business owners, and humans, we are surrounded by ongoing change whether or not we acknowledge it. Change cannot be stopped. Rather than be stymied by it, we can use design thinking principles and tools to help us meet head-on the challenges and opportunities spawned by change, prepared and unafraid. From large-scale change that affects entire economies or smaller-scale change that affects only our businesses, designing our response to change enables us not only to tolerate it but also embrace it.

# Designing for Growth

## Minimize Growing Pains

By no means can growth be pain-free; it isn't a reasonable expectation to think that could be possible. Think back to when you were a child and your arms and legs would occasionally—and seemingly randomly—ache for no apparent reason. If your mother was like mine, she described those aches as growing pains. If you were like I was, that answer seemed like the dumbest thing you had ever heard. Worse, you were powerless to prevent the ache.

When it comes to business, growing is accompanied by occasional aches and pains, just like in childhood. But with forethought and the purposeful application of design thinking tools that accommodate and embrace growth, you can minimize the growing pains and put your business and team in a position to capitalize on every opportunity that comes your way.

---

▨ **Note**  You can't prevent growing pains, but you can minimize them by using design thinking practices.

---

## Why Growth Is Important

Growing a business can be overwhelming, intimidating, and challenging. It can be exhilarating and rewarding. It should also be a constant.

Many of us will reach a point at which we are satisfied with the volume of business we conduct with the size of company we have and in the markets in which we operate. Reaching a point of satisfaction is a milestone that can and should be celebrated! However, without some continuing degree of growth, that milestone could turn into a gravestone. Growth is one of the key factors that keeps your business alive and thriving.

It's imperative to understand that the opposite of growth is not stability. It isn't even stagnation. The opposite of growth is loss. We do not live in a static world; change is a constant and it surrounds us all the time. My contention is that unless your business continually grows, you will experience loss. Let's use a forest as an example.

A forest is composed of many trees, all of which are growing at varying rates. Is there a point at which all the trees decide that they are tall enough and just stop growing? No. Their growth is constant. Imagine, though, that one tree—we'll call him George—decides that enough is enough, and he's through with this growing stuff. He's worked hard the past few decades to get where he is today—an admirably tall tree with well-formed, lush branches that attract many birds to nest there: the very definition of a successful tree. George is satisfied and happy and is ready to rest easy and enjoy the results of his growth.

Meanwhile, George's neighbor trees keep growing. George notices small changes over the years as the other trees grow while he stays the same: some of the birds didn't return to nest, and he doesn't seem to be getting as much sunlight as before. As more time passes, those changes become more profound: less and less sunlight reaches through the branches above him on the trees that kept growing, making it very difficult to maintain his leafy, lush branches. His only wildlife residents are a pair of squirrels; the birds left for other trees and branches where the sun is brighter. Clearly, George isn't thriving as he once was. He has lost his successful place amid the forest.

George realizes that to regain his previous success, he needs to grow, although now he'll have to catch up to the neighbor trees. He notices that even the neighbor tree that seemed to be going nowhere is still taller and lusher than he, because it kept growing.

Will George be able to grow and catch up to the forest that surrounds him? Maybe, maybe not. What if he had kept growing? Even at a small rate, he would have continued to grow enough to at least keep up with the neighbor trees and not have lost his access to the resources he needed to sustain himself.

I am not advocating for a "keeping up with the Joneses" approach to business. What I am suggesting is that you recognize that a degree of growth is mandatory for sustainable business success. If you choose not to grow, you also choose to tolerate the inevitable loss.

# Growing Gracefully

In this chapter, I recommend several design thinking activities geared toward embracing growth and growing your business at a modest rate. I believe that this is where the greater challenge lies. Rapid growth—that of the start-up variety—is an entirely different dynamic and probably one with which you as an entrepreneur and business owner are familiar.

I abhor the adage, "Hindsight is twenty-twenty." It's usually proffered in a rueful kind of way, and that isn't helpful. However, the concept behind the adage has merit. Looking back at our history and mining that information for what has worked—and made us successful—in the past is a great starting point when designing for growth.

If your business is growing in staff size or expanding its current operating capacity, reviewing and documenting past events and successes as well as failures and missteps becomes an important process for charting effective growth. Visualizing that history aids your team in discovering, recognizing, articulating, appreciating, and potentially replicating the key components of what got the business to where it is today. The 20-20 exercise guides you in mapping those components and using them as a roadmap for future growth.

# Hindsight Is 20-20

You can conduct the 20-20 exercise with as few as five people or as many as fifty. It is an accommodating format for larger groups, which is a rather uncommon feature among design thinking activities. Gather what you now know to be the requisite white board or flip charts, and the appropriate marker type, and several stacks of sticky notes. This exercise doesn't require an outside moderator, so you can lead it yourself.

Start by drawing a continuous horizontal line across the width of the white board. If you're using flip-chart paper, you'll want to hang several pieces—end-to-end horizontally—to accommodate your line. This is your timeline. Several factors affect how you label. If yours is a young company, you might label the left end point with the year you started the company, and then mark the rest of in one-year increments. If yours is a more established company, you might label the left end point with the date of a key moment, like the year you launched a new product, and mark the rest of the timeline in five-year increments. There is no rule to follow other than label your timeline in a way that is relevant to your business.

Since we started this chapter illustrating the concept of growth with a forest, let's use a plant nursery that's been in business for six years as our example for the 20-20 activity. As with other activities, you should consider recording the session. The nursery's timeline would start with the year the business launched, say, 2005, with one-year increments (Figure 9-1). Be sure to leave plenty of space above and below the time-line and between each labeled increment, to allow for notes and written comments.

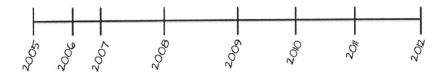

Joe's Nursery

**Figure 9-1.** 20-20 timeline

---

■ **Tip**    If there are years during which your business experienced significant changes, allow a little extra space than for other years.

---

Next, ask each participant to write his or her name and one or two words about their first impressions of the company on a sticky note, and post it on the timeline below the year that person joined the company (Figure 9-2). If you have a group of fewer than twelve, ask each person to share a brief story about joining the company as they post. Additionally, if your group includes staff that has been with the company since the beginning, pay especially close attention to their stories. Their historical perspective of the business is invaluable to this process.

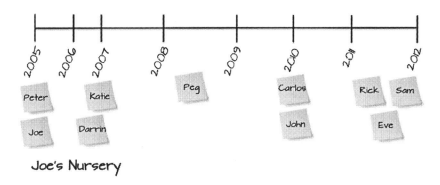

Joe's Nursery

**Figure 9-2.** 20-20 timeline with team added

Now ask your team questions, and flesh out the map by capturing their answers—using text and images—on sticky notes and placing them at the appropriate points along the timeline (Figure 9-3). Encourage your team to provide as many answers as they can, but remember, just one answer or response per note. Potential topics could include the following:

1. Company successes

2. Company missteps

3. Lessons learned

4. Changes in leadership

5. Changes in mission, vision, or values

6. Changes in product or service offerings

7. Market trends

8. Competitive shifts

9. Major client acquisitions or losses

10. Shifts in revenue

11. Shifts in staff size

12. Major client projects

13. Internal reorganizations

14. Technology developments

15. Regulatory or legal changes

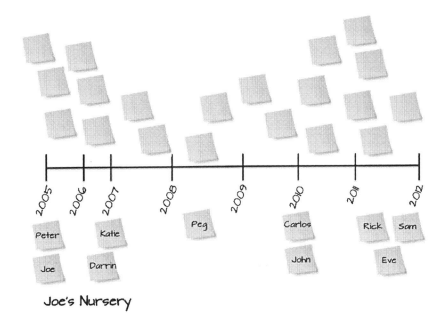

**Figure 9-3.** 20-20 timeline with team input

If you really want to be organized for this activity, consider assigning specific colors of sticky notes to represent categories of answers. For example, internal topics could be yellow, market-based and external topics could be blue, and lessons learned could be pink.

As you add sticky notes to the timeline, ask open-ended questions to stimulate thinking and keep the conversation going. Encourage storytelling and honesty, even about the hard times. If the process stalls, try reenergizing it with observations of your own.

---

▓ **Tip** If you aren't comfortable drawing—or feel like you can't draw—then come up with some recognizable icons before the meeting. Visuals will aid the process and provide quick points of reference.

---

Once you have captured the group's answers, summarize the information on the timeline and ask the group to identify patterns, share what they have learned, and say how they can leverage this information and perspective for the company's continued growth. You many need to ask questions to prompt the conversation. Some of those could be:

- How have these patterns influenced the development of the company?

- What is the most important lesson we have learned?

- At what point was the company most successful, and why?

To conclude the 20-20 activity, ask your team to think about the company's next steps moving forward. What is the most important thing the company can do next to capitalize on its history and leverage it for future success? Leave your timeline posted and have each participant post a response to your question at the far right end during the remainder of the day, and reconvene briefly at the end of the day to review them. Be sure to take photos of the final, completed timeline so you can refer back to it as needed.

# Designing New Hires

Inevitably, with growth comes ambiguity. Leadership has a general idea of what they want and/or need as the company grows, but often it is difficult to define and clearly articulate. This applies to the growth of a company's business operations, including product and service development, and also to the growth of its business support, namely, its staff. During a growth phase, you might know you need a new vice president of sales, but what does that mean to you? Sure, you can draft a job description that uses all of the key terms that a recruit would expect to see, but is that the best approach to sourcing the right person—not just the right skill set—to fill the role?

As powerful as design thinking is, its tools and activities are predominantly geared toward solving problems and meeting challenges in all aspects of business except those that are human. I find that puzzling because the largest expense for small businesses isn't rent or production costs but payroll. Because of this, staffing deserves (and frankly is overdue for) a little design thinking love. To that end, I've adapted the Design the Box activity to address a business's needs to grow its staff.

Normally, Design the Box is focused on developing a new product or service for a business from the perspective of first designing the box in which the product—or metaphorical box for a service—is delivered.

The premise of the exercise is that if you design the box first, you can better articulate the features, benefits, and unique selling points that need to be embodied in the product.[1]

For the purpose of applying design thinking to staffing needs, let's call this exercise Design the VP, because the example I'll use our example the plant nursery's need for a new vice president of sales. (If you needed to hire a new art director, you would call the exercise Design the Art Director.) Just change the name of the exercise to include the position for which you are hiring, and you're set.

Start the Design the VP activity just as you would the Design the Box activity: with defining what is "in" the VP. On a white board or flip chart, draw the shape of a person in the center. I draw a stick figure, because that is the extent of my artistic talent. At the top of the page, write the title of the position for which you are designing (Figure 9-4).

VP of Sales

Joe's Nursery

**Figure 9-4.** Design the VP starting point

---

[1] There's a great example of Design the Box shared by Kate Verrill online. See http://www.gogamestorm.com/?p=576.

Using the plant nursery example as the one hiring the VP, we determine the qualities that need to be in the VP and list those near the corresponding area of the stick figure. For example, we might determine that the VP needs to be articulate and communicate well, so we draw a speech bubble near the figure's head and include those descriptors (Figure 9-5).

**Figure 9-5.** Design the VP in progress

We might decide that the VP needs to have a college degree and previous sales experience, so we add those features to the figure. We might decide that our VP needs have experience with plants, so add that feature, too. (Figure 9-6).

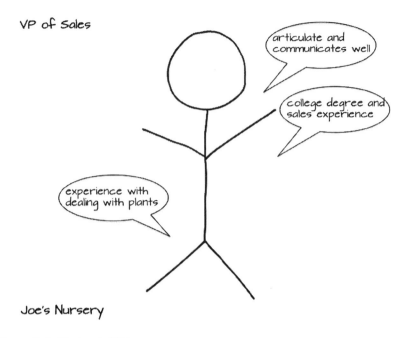

VP of Sales

articulate and communicates well

college degree and sales experience

experience with dealing with plants

Joe's Nursery

**Figure 9-6.** Design the VP in progress

Once we've defined what we need "in" our VP, we need to design the VP itself. Rather than designing a prototype of a box, like we would in the Design the Box activity, we're going to design the person in Design the VP. We will articulate what about the person's personality and presence we want and need for a VP. Imagine the process of interviewing live candidates for this position: what would influence you to choose one candidate over another beyond what is on his or her résumé?

---

▧ **Note** Do not let designing the person spark controversy. Keep physical descriptions and specific attributes out of the conversation!

---

For the VP of sales at the plant nursery, we might decide that we want someone who smiles easily and genuinely, so we add that to the stick figure. We may decide also that the person needs to be able to make cold calls comfortably and can work equally well with corporate clients and landscape companies, so we add those features, too (Figure 9-7).

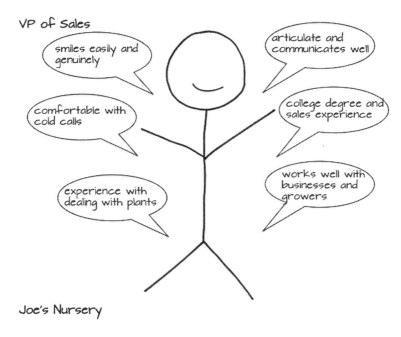

**Figure 9-7.** Design the VP completed

Now we have a visual representation of the type of person with the skill set and attributes we want for the position. We can use that as a touchstone as we recruit and interview candidates, ensuring that they meet the requirements we designed. Did we design a man or a woman? A blonde or a redhead? Single or married? None of those attributes matter, nor can they legally guide hiring practices.

# Cross-Pollinating Ideas

One of the more common areas of business growth, and perhaps one of the most fun, is expanding the products or services your company offers. Ideation alone generates a lot of interest among and participation from staff. However, the process of expanding a product or service line closely mirrors the overall design thinking process, and you must perform due diligence for understanding and defining the need and potential opportunity before you jump into ideation. Assuming you've done that and are ready to start brainstorming ways to innovate and expand on what your company offers, I suggest introducing your team to a design thinking technique called heuristic ideation.

Heuristic ideation is a rather fancy way of saying "rapid brainstorming." The technique speeds up the process of generating ideas by associating concepts disparate to one another but still relevant to the bigger picture. And it is a lot of fun.

As with all design thinking activities, you need a white board or flip chart and markers. Sticky notes are optional for this one! The first step is to determine what you want to brainstorm about and two descriptive attributes that you can use to define the matrix. For the plant nursery example, we might populate the matrix with a look at plant usage (interiors, exteriors, and events) and contract duration (purchase, long-term rental, short-term rental). On the board, draw a matrix and populate it with our information (Figure 9-8).

| Joe's Nursery | Interiors | Exteriors | Events |
|---|---|---|---|
| Purchase | | | |
| Long-term Contract | | | |
| Short-term Contract | | | |

**Figure 9-8.** Rapid brainstorming matrix

---

**Note** The rapid brainstorming matrix can be any size, but I recommend nothing larger than six cells by six cells.

---

During the activity, the group looks across the cells for unusual or unexpected combinations to spark new ideas. Some of the combinations may not make sense at first, but they could contain a nugget of an idea worth exploring, or they could trigger other thoughts that lead to more viable possibilities. There may be some combinations for which the group cannot come up with any compelling ideas. In those instances, you may want to add another attribute to add to the matrix or alter the attributes already in the matrix (Figure 9-9).

| Joe's Nursery | Interiors | Exteriors | Events |
|---|---|---|---|
| Purchase | Shopping malls, offices, schools, hotels, hospitals | Shopping malls, parks, offices, apartments | Theme parks, festival grounds, event venues |
| Long-term Contract | Offices, hotels, hospitals, museums | Parks, model homes, showrooms | ??? |
| Short-term Contract | ??? | Farmers Markets, food truck parks | Galas, fundraising events, conventions, conferences |

**Figure 9-9.** Rapid brainstorming matrix complete

Once you've generated as many cross-pollinated ideas as possible, have the group assess which two are the most viable and explore how to prototype those ideas. At that point, you'll be on the path to determining if your growth plan can include those new ideas.

# Summary

Growth is an integral part of business, whether it is incremental, monumental, or somewhere in between. It can take on a wide variety of forms, be localized in specific departments or niches of your business, or sweep through your entire organization, leaving no area unaffected. Quite plainly, growth happens. With design thinking tools, you'll be equipped to anticipate opportunities, embrace growth, and purposefully direct your efforts and resources in a way that will best benefit your business in the long run.

# Case Studies
## Design Thinking in Action

Putting design thinking into action might feel like second nature or the most foreign thing on the planet, but it's happening every day in large corporate boardrooms and in break-out sessions at conferences around the world. Design thinking isn't just for big businesses, though, as you've discovered through the previous chapters. Many small businesses owners and entrepreneurs have dipped their toes in the design thinking water and have applied its principles to a variety of challenges.

Following are examples of success stories with small organizations' first forays into working with design thinking activities and exercises. The case studies cover a variety of situations to give you the broadest view into how design thinking has been used by others much like you.

Come on in; the water's fine.

## Design Thinking and Branding Strategy

Innovation in technology is booming with no discernible end in sight. There are thousands upon thousands of entrepreneurs and small businesses entering that space, particularly in the area of mobile application development and design, where they are producing hundreds of thousands of products. With that much activity, the mobile application landscape is always changing. When introducing a new application, creating distinctive branding is critical, but equally critical is getting it done quickly.

An integrated marketing and web strategy firm based on the East Coast had an idea for a mobile app that would fill a niche and provide an innovative solution for professional and hobbyist photographers and filmmakers. After a thorough review of mobile apps already available, the firm determined that it had a viable idea and proceeded to use their internal resources to develop the application.

Once the app was bug-free, the firm was ready to brand it. I led the firm's senior leadership through a Microscoping brand DNA exercise (see Chapter 7) to identify, describe, and coalesce around the key features of the application's brand, the brand's personality, and the brand's core.

Ideally, the Microscoping exercise is done in person on a white board or flip chart. Because of budget restraints, I stayed in my office in Texas, while the firm's leadership stayed in their office on the East Coast, and we used an online collaborative workspace and conference calls to complete the exercise. Although we were successful, conducting Microscoping remotely would never be my first recommendation. Unless there is a greatly compelling reason not to gather the group in the same physical space, opt for the in-person version of the exercise.

As we worked through the exercise, we discovered that the firm's senior leadership held disparate viewpoints in two of the seven areas of the brand's DNA, including the core. Through some honest conversation, we were able to come to an agreement and a shared definition of those two areas. We accomplished what we set out to do: create a well-defined brand DNA that would guide all branding efforts for the application moving forward (see Figure A-1).

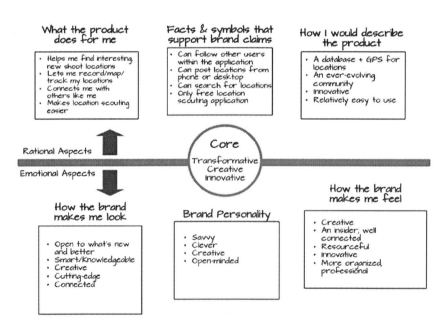

**Figure A-1.** Microscoping brand DNA chart

Had we not used the Microscoping exercise and uncovered the disparities among the leadership team, we potentially could have made strategic errors in developing a marketing strategy and plan for the application that could have led to a loss of opportunity, time, and resources.

As the app has continued to develop and accommodate user needs, the brand has stayed true to its DNA, continues to communicate to its target audiences in terms that support the brand as well as resonate with its targets, and consistently adds new users—all indicators that the Microscoping exercise was successful in defining the brand accurately and meaningfully.

## CASE STUDY SNAPSHOT

Challenge: Develop a solid, relevant brand strategy for a new mobile application developed by an interactive marketing and web strategy firm.

Action: Using the Microscoping brand DNA exercise, identify and articulate the seven aspects of the brand: what it does, how a user would describe it, facts and symbols to support brand claims, how a user perceives others' opinions of him when using the brand, how the brand makes the user feel, the brand's personality, and the core tenets of the brand.

Result: A well-defined, sustainable brand DNA profile created collaboratively and wholly adopted by the firm's senior leadership.

# Design Thinking and Business Strategy

Regardless of your viewpoint of health care in America, you have to admit that it is ripe for innovation. (Whether you can navigate your way through the complexity of the system is another matter.) No other industry in the past decade has stood at the precipice of such massive, sweeping change that will affect every individual and business in the country. Even the largest health care providers are having difficulty tackling the challenges that face them.

One of those providers saw an opportunity for innovation in the health care marketplace that greatly would benefit the American consumer, yet its senior leadership knew that it would not be able to capitalize on that opportunity in a successful way within its current organizational structure. In true entrepreneurial spirit, that company spawned a separate health care start-up to shepherd a new business concept to fill the innovation gap.

The start-up's leadership needed innovative thought partners to help them develop the new company's business model, organizational structure, and operations processes that would launch the business. They engaged a firm of which I was part of the senior leadership and would spearhead the initiative with one of the firm's partners.

At the outset, the company's only asset was an idea on a page from a yellow notepad. As monumental as the idea was—to create a service that helps patients navigate the health care industry—no implementation plan or organizational structure existed to bring the initiative to life. Our first application of design thinking principles came in the form of Stakeholder Visioning (see Chapter 3). The start-up's leadership comprised very senior, exceptionally knowledgeable, and experienced health care executives, which translated into a lot of brainpower. It also translated into some difficulty in shifting mindsets and adopting the perspective of stakeholders other than health care providers. The start-up's business idea included both consumer-facing and provider-facing services, so the need to fully capture the perspectives of both stakeholder groups was imperative.

We had to balance the wants and needs of competing interests during this exercise. To do so effectively, we had to check our assumptions and our perceived business constraints at the door. The experienced health care leaders would have to think like consumers without considering whether their business (or any other) could fulfill what the consumers wanted and needed.

Although the Stakeholder Vision exercise was a challenge at first, we successfully completed the process and used its outcomes to define the start-up's business model, organizational structure, operating processes, mission, vision, and values to all parties' satisfaction—and within thirty days of the legal formation of the company.

## CASE STUDY SNAPSHOT

Challenge: Develop a viable business strategy, organizational structure, and operating processes for a health care start-up.

Action: Using Stakeholder Visioning, identify the needs and wants of two key stakeholders—health care consumers and providers—and appropriately balance them to develop a business model that not only meets consumer expectations but also is sustainable by and profitable for providers.

Result: A solid foundation on which it could build its service offerings and brand strategy and from which the start-up could launch into the marketplace.

# Design Thinking and Customer Experience

Retail is no easy business, yet it makes up several vertebrae in our country's economic backbone. According to U.S. Census data from 2010, there are nearly 6 million retail trade firms in the country, more than 5 million of which have twenty or fewer employees.[1] That is a lot of competition in a small business marketplace. Distinguishing your business is imperative for success—nay, survival—and one means of doing so is through the purposeful design of the customer experience.

A franchisee of a specialty running retailer in the South had seen competition in her market steadily increase over the span of two years. Although her store was still performing well, she wanted to ensure that she kept her current customer base engaged and satisfied, as well as attracting new customers, whom she could convert into loyal ones. In sum, she wanted to deliver a memorable and pleasing in-store experience to her customers.

A review of the previous year's sales activity revealed that the product category that underperformed most significantly was apparel. In fact, although apparel occupied more than 50 percent of the store's square footage, apparel sales accounted for less than 15 percent of total sales. Not only did this directly affect the store's profitability, but also—and more important to the franchisee—the customer was missing the full experience of shopping in the store. The big question before the franchisee and her leadership team was, "Why aren't customers shopping apparel?"

To uncover the root answer to that question, we used The 5 Whys activity (see Chapter 2), during which we all sounded like toddlers asking, "Why?" We started with the premise, "Our customers aren't shopping the whole store," and proceeded through asking ourselves "why?" repeatedly in an effort to peel back the layers of perception and get to the root. With each "why?" we dug deeper into the answer, ultimately arriving at the response, "Because we aren't promoting it or talking about it. And those areas of the store are dark" (see Figure A-2).

---

[1] See http://www.census.gov/econ/susb/index.html.

# Our customers aren't shopping the whole store.

**Why?** ➡ Because they're focused on getting new shoes. They aren't looking around the store, just making a beeline for the shoe wall.

**Why?** ➡ They know us best for shoes. They aren't used to buying other stuff at our store.

**Why?** ➡ They go to other stores to buy other products, like apparel.

**Why?** ➡ They don't know what kind of other stuff we have. They see it, but walk by it.

**Why?** ➡ Because we aren't promoting it or talking about it. And those areas of the store are dark.

**Figure A-2.** The 5 Whys chart

Prior to any experience design work, I spent a half-day in the store observing customers and their shopping behavior, and conducting the Customer Intercepts research exercise. Nearly 90 percent of customers didn't shop the entire store. They went directly to the shoe wall display. Of the customers who did shop beyond the shoe wall, the recovery equipment display in the front of the store by the showcase window attracted the most attention. The common denominator of both areas: they are well lit. Among the varying reasons customers provided for why they didn't shop the other areas in the store were these nuggets: they didn't notice the other areas, the apparel didn't catch their eye, and that part of the store just didn't seem appealing. Although the customers didn't exactly say, "That part of the store is dark," their answers seemed to support the answer to the fifth why in the exercise.

That was our lightbulb moment, figuratively and literally. The information from the customer intercepts and observational research revealed that customers weren't getting the in-store experience the franchisee wanted to deliver because the apparel wasn't showcased or merchandised effectively. One means of correction that was in franchisee' sphere of control was to improve the lighting and how the apparel was merchandised so that the light drew the customers' eyes to the displays.

Sixty days after the changes were made, we followed with another review of sales data and another series of customer intercepts. The data showed increases in apparel sales, and the customer feedback was more positive about the in-store experience, citing not only the apparel displays but also a general, overall feeling of lightness, energy, and color.

---

**CASE STUDY SNAPSHOT**

Challenge: Design and deliver an in-store experience that would engage customers in a meaningful way, while also guiding them to shop the entire store, rather than one or two specific areas.

Action: Using The 5 Whys activity, ask iterative, probing questions to identify the root cause of why customers were not shopping the entire store, which resulted in a less-than-desirable customer experience.

Result: A specific, actionable, and manageable plan for design modifications to the store that would result in a better customer experience and potentially improved category sales.

---

# Design Thinking and Change

When you've had a successful business for more than two decades, it's easy to fall into predictable patterns. Although you shouldn't scoff at or undermine solid processes and best practices, too much routine can leave your business stale and potentially bore your target audiences.

A singer/songwriter/guitarist based in the Midwest had enjoyed twenty-plus years of success with radio airplay, opening national tour dates for A-list acts, and filling concert halls coast to coast. As with any business, though, he was experiencing a valley among his hills—a downward trend in ticket sales—and wanted to mitigate that as quickly as possible. That trend was a reflection of a target audience that had subtly changed while the singer was preoccupied with handling the day-to-day tasks of being a professional musician. He couldn't see the forest for the trees. We met his challenge head-on with the Forest and Trees exercise (Chapter 8).

When the singer, his manager, and I launched into the Forest and Trees exercise, we knew full well we would identify dozens of trees. However, none of us knew what the forest would hold. At the end of the exercise, we had uncovered the following themes in both the trees and forest sections: touring, funding, and branding. The most compelling realization was this: the singer's primary target audience had aged with him, and this fact had ramifications in all three themed areas. The singer and his fan base were no longer in their twenties, with disposable income and few responsibilities. They were now in their forties, with children, mortgages, and limited free time. With the realization that the target audience had changed significantly came the realization that the singer's brand had not.

Now that we could see the forest, we could take deliberate steps toward designing for this change that had affected the singer's business. Although his brand still resonated strongly with his target audience, it wasn't connecting with younger consumers. This was our problem to solve using the 3-12-3 activity, also described in Chapter 8, the outcomes of which included a shift in strategic planning for the singer's next concert season, as well as a shift in his brand DNA. As of this writing, those shifts had occurred and the singer is seeing greater diversity among his audiences, as well as performing at festivals and venues that generally attract a younger demographic.

---

### CASE STUDY SNAPSHOT

Challenge: Evaluate the business landscape to determine how to best design for and adapt to changes in the market and among the target audience.

Action: Using the Forest and Trees exercise and the 3-12-3 activity, identify the most relevant and actionable means to mitigate the negative effects of change and capitalize on opportunities.

Result: Appropriate shifts in the business's strategic plan and brand DNA to accommodate the change.

---

# Design Thinking and Research

Launching a new business takes guts. Launching one in an industry suffering through the throes of frequent change takes guts and blind faith. However, neither pays the bills or generates profits. Research prior to planning and launch will save you time, effort, money, and headaches. As entrepreneurs, we get excited about ideas and opportunities, and we might rush to implement them and realize success. No more! It's time to make a commitment to research and due diligence before action.

The former editor of a printed alternative news source made a path-altering choice and moved to editing an online-only alternative news source of her own creation. She had gathered a plethora of research in the form of competitive analyses, business models, and market demographics—all sources of secondary quantitative data. Feeling confident that she had created a marketable product, she launched the online source to rave reviews.

After an initial period of rapid growth, the news source's readership and paid subscriber base leveled out. A review of the source's content, design, and delivery mechanisms assured the editor that all was aligned with the data she had collected. However, the picture wasn't complete without qualitative data.

Rather than experimenting with format and content in an attempt to reenergize the acquisition of readers and paid subscribers, the editor engaged my services to conduct qualitative research with current subscribers for the purpose of using the information to fine-tune her product offering. The usual approaches to qualitative research, covered in Chapter 2, require face-to-face contact. Unfortunately, we faced two significant challenges to traditional qualitative research: for the majority of the subscriber base, the editor had only email addresses, and the start-up nature of the venture demanded the process be quick and inexpensive.

The answer to these challenges would be an amalgam of quantitative and qualitative research techniques. We used a customizable survey instrument that could be delivered through email, and we employed qualitative questioning formats and techniques used in customer intercepts and one-on-one interviews to design the survey's content. Not only did this approach solve the challenge with reaching the subscriber base, it was delivered quickly and at a very low cost. The resulting hybrid research tool was successful. More than 25 percent of paid subscribers responded to the survey (average response rate is 15 percent), providing richly detailed information and unique perspectives that proved helpful in guiding the editor in her product refinement.

## CASE STUDY SNAPSHOT

Challenge: Uncover the reasons behind the start-up's sluggish growth and look for ways to modify the business's product appropriately.

Action: Using a hybrid of quantitative and qualitative research techniques, elicit detailed information from participants solely through an online delivery mechanism.

Result: A higher-than-average response rate with subscribers providing in-depth opinions and perspectives that would inform the product's future development.

# Metrics for Design Thinking

## Measuring Performance

Every bit of work and every penny invested are for nothing if you aren't measuring their return. It's a core tenet of operating a profitable, successful business. The same rule applies for design thinking initiatives: you must measure.

Metrics—the measurements by which you gauge an initiative's success or failure (or other characteristics)—need to be one of your best friends, yet they are hard to get to know. They can seem aloof, elusive, oppositional, and secretive. In reality, they are eager to be transparent and give you everything they have.

As business owners and entrepreneurs, we face two distinct challenges when it comes to metrics: identifying the relevant ones and taking the time to measure them over multiple periods. That's just for the metrics of the processes with which we are familiar. Introduce design thinking into the mix—new approaches to problem solving with which you may not be familiar—and you might think you need a whole new set of metrics.

This is not necessarily the case.

Many of the ways you normally measure progress can also be used to measure design thinking–based initiatives: foot traffic, inquiries, sales, referrals, impressions, click-throughs, content subscriptions, page views, follows and likes, satisfaction ratings, and churn. All of these measurements are applicable depending on the circumstance.

# Relevant Metrics

Following is a brief reference guide to use in helping you and your leadership team determine what measurement to use when.

## Foot Traffic

Uniquely relevant for retailers and public spaces, such as libraries and parks, foot traffic is measured by simply counting the number of individuals who enter your space within a specified timeframe. Measuring foot traffic is as easy—and as boring as—standing by a door and using a hand-held tally counter. If your marketing plan is designed to increase the number of visitors to your store, measuring foot traffic will give you insight into the plan's success.

## Inquiries

Prompting a customer to inquire about additional information is a call-to-action tactic often used by businesses with a long sales process or complex products. Inquiries are also a means of gauging a customer's level of interest in a product or service. You can measure inquiries by tracking the mechanism you created for generating them in your call to action, for example, phone calls, emails, coupons redeemed, and so on.

## Sales

This is likely the most popular measurement and one of the easiest to track. However, sales are not always an accurate reflection of an initiative's success. Many other factors can affect sales: availability of inventory, cost, employee interaction, fulfillment, and so on. Although sales are generally considered the ultimate measure of success, that metric should never be the only measure.

## Referrals

New customers referred by current ones or by vendors—customers who come to you via word of mouth—are highly desirable by any business. To measure referrals through customer interaction, whether in person or on the phone, you can simply ask the customer how he or she heard about your business. Customer referrals through the Internet can be tracked using web analytics (see Appendix C for a definition).

# Impressions

Measuring impressions is often referred to as "counting eyeballs," because one Impression is equivalent to one person seeing one piece of communication (advertisement, web page, billboard, and so on) one time. Marketing communication is almost exclusively measured by impressions. Impressions can be measured in several ways. Print media measures impressions based on circulation and distribution counts. Broadcast media measures impressions based on data reported by listeners or viewers through services such as Nielsen. Impressions for online media are measured by unique IP addresses.

# Click-Throughs

This is a means of measuring web-based communication specifically. A click-through is the action someone takes when they click on an advertisement or a link embedded in one piece of communication that takes the reader to another piece of communication, for example, a link from a retailer's e-newsletter to the retailer's product page.

# Content Subscriptions

A click-through is occasionally followed by an opportunity to subscribe to a company's newsletter. If one of your goals is to increase your database of customers and potential customers to whom you can communicate regularly, use this metric.

# Page Views

A click-through can also be followed by a page view. A page view is a specific type of impression, measured by tracking unique IP addresses. It is the equivalent of one person viewing one page on your website one time. Page views are a common metric for measuring a website's traffic.

# Follows and Likes

In the realm of social media, "follows" and "likes" are the primary means of measuring customer engagement. On Facebook, users "like" businesses. On Twitter, Instagram, Pinterest, and similar platforms, users "follow" businesses.

## Satisfaction Ratings

Rating satisfaction with a business, whether among employees or customers, is a common practice. The rub is that this metric requires a baseline to measure against, so satisfaction must be measured twice before results can be meaningful. The most common means of measurement are surveys, which can be delivered online, via phone, or through the regular mail, and customer comment forms.

## Churn

This has nothing to do with butter. Churn, also called churn rate or attrition rate, refers to the rate at which a business loses customers. Churn is measured during a defined timeframe, and although it is a metric most commonly used by subscription-based business models, like mobile phones and magazines, it can be relevant to any business sector that tracks the purchase history and behavior of its customers. If the life cycle of your product or service is three months, and a customer hasn't made a repeat purchase within nine months of his or her initial purchase, you've probably lost that customer.

# When to Measure Performance

Many clients have asked me when they should measure performance. My pat answer is "Always." In all seriousness, keeping your finger on the pulse of your business by measuring relevant metrics regularly is good business. Getting into the habit will help you identify potential challenges and opportunities while they are still on the horizon so you can prepare for their arrival.

If measuring performance is new for you, select relevant metrics that you can measure at a frequency that will be not only meaningful but also feasible. Some business sectors benefit from daily or evenly hourly measuring, others suffice with monthly or quarterly measurements. At the absolute minimum, take measurements of relevant metrics at least annually, which could be at the end or beginning of your fiscal year, or on your business anniversary date ... essentially any date that makes sense for you.

From a design thinking point of view, I firmly believe that regardless of your ongoing measurements, you also need to measure before and after any design thinking initiative. It's logical and necessary if you want to gauge results accurately. For example, if you are going to redesign your store to increase foot traffic, you should measure that foot traffic prior to the redesign. Also measure the foot traffic afterward at three regular intervals so that you have an average foot traffic count, which you can then compare to the result you obtained before the redesign.

# Measurement and the Iterative Nature of Design Thinking

By its very nature design thinking is an iterative process that perfectly illustrates the saying, "If at first you don't succeed, try, try again." Hence, design thinking includes prototyping and testing as critical steps in the process. Those of us who use design thinking in our businesses know that rarely (f ever) will we get it right the first time, regardless of what "it" is. There is and always will be room for improvement, so we prototype and test as many times as necessary to get the results we want. Therein lies the core reason that measurement is hugely important not only in business but also in design thinking. Knowing the results of our efforts aids us in making adjustments quickly so we can try again, and again, until we get it right.

# Glossary of Design Thinking Jargon

## Put the Right Words in Your Mouth

I have never played Meeting Bingo—the game you can play secretly during a meeting when you're bored. It's played like bingo, but instead of keeping track of B-5 and O-70, you keep track of jargon and business-speak like "parking lot this issue" and "sustainable practices." We've all been in meetings like that, and they validate my belief that jargon should be banned from any gathering of two or more professionals.

Since the likelihood of that happening is slim to none, I want to arm you with the definitions of the most common design thinking jargon so that you can talk the talk with the best of them.

## Common Design Thinking Terminology

**Co-creation:** the development of creating a product, service, or process by more than one stakeholder group; see *also* Collaborative

**Collaborative:** two or more stakeholder groups combine inputs, ideas, and insights to create a product, service, or process; see *also* Co-creation

**Context:** the circumstances in which an idea, event, or decision exists and which can influence the outcome

**Culture of Collaboration:** purposefully designed business culture that values collaboration across teams, departments, and business sectors

**Customer Engagement:** the act of connecting a customer to a brand, business, or other customer with the purpose of provoking conversation and feedback

**Customer Experience:** whether online or in person, the experience a customer has when interacting with your brand, business, and employees

**Deep Design:** design with the purpose of appealing not only to the conscious mind but also to the subconscious

**Design Strategy:** the process of applying design thinking principles to business strategy, incorporating research and holistic thinking; the intersection of design and strategic planning

**Digital Storytelling:** sharing via digital media a business's compelling, meaningful story intended to build a connection with target audiences; see *also* Storytelling

**Empathy:** understanding another's feelings, thoughts, or attitudes; a requirement for developing communications, experiences, and interactions with target audiences

**Experience Design:** the process of applying design thinking principles to create a meaningful experience for customers, employees, or other pertinent stakeholders

**Feedback Loop:** a system through which customers, employees, and other pertinent stakeholders can share insights, opinions, thoughts, and criticisms directly to a business; a process through which information flows forward as well as feeds back on itself

**Futurists:** consultants, organizational leaders, strategists, and others who use design thinking, systems thinking, and other interdisciplinary approaches to anticipate economic, social, and political changes that could affect business

**Getting Traction:** making progress toward strategic business objectives

**Human Capital:** the collection of skills, abilities, expertise, and creativity among a business's employees and senior leadership that can be leveraged to produce economic value

**Ideation:** the fourth step in the design thinking process; the act of generating ideas in a rapid manner without regard for constraints; brainstorming

**Ideograph:** *also* Ideogram; a symbol or picture used to represent an idea, concept, or thing in place of a word, or when there isn't a word to use accurately in the symbol's place

**Integrated Thinking:** an approach to thinking that balances multiple constraints and evaluates the potential effect of those constraints as the balance shifts

**Intrapreneur:** being or behaving like an entrepreneur from within an organization

**Iterate:** to repeat a process or action, making modifications along the way, with the purpose of reaching a desired outcome

**Key Performance Indicators (KPIs):** a defined and specific metric by which performance is measured; also called benchmarks or milestones

**Mind Map:** a nonlinear diagram used to visually outline information; often centered on a word or short phrase that represents a concept, challenge, or opportunity; associated words, ideas, and concepts are then added around the center

**Prototype:** a sample, model, or work-in-progress of a product, service, or process used for testing viability and gathering stakeholder input

**Radical Innovation:** innovation on such a grand or unpredicted scale that it disrupts an entire industry; often driven by an idea instead of customer need

**Roadmap:** an outline that often uses visuals to depict how a business will proceed from a starting point to reach a defined objective

**Scenario Planning:** a flexible means of strategic planning that accommodates two or more "if-then" situations that allows a business to anticipate and prepare for varying versions of the future

**Social Entrepreneur:** an individual who takes an entrepreneurial approach to developing scalable solutions to social problems

**Social Innovation:** the act of using innovation processes to help solve social challenges; can also refer to specific innovations that have a social purpose, for example, microcredit

**Stakeholders:** groups that have some degree of interest in the general operations, successes, and failures of a business, such as customers, employees, and so on

**Storytelling:** sharing a business's key messages and story in a predominantly narrative format intended to build emotional connections between the business and stakeholders

**User-Centered Design:** an approach to design that considers the needs and wants of the end users of a product or service at each stage of the process; multistage problem solving that requires designers to anticipate the desires of end users and test their assumptions

**User-Centered Research:** research to determine the needs and wants of the end users of a product or service with the purpose of designing it to more accurately meet those needs and wants; may include research to test the ability of an existing product or service to meet those needs and wants

**User Experience (UX):** refers to the quality of the interaction between a person and a piece of technology or software, with particular attention paid to ease of use and efficiency; the outcome of user-centered research and design

**Visual Thinking:** a means of communicating thoughts and ideas through symbols and imagery; often used during brainstorming or ideation sessions; also called graphic recording, visual notes, or sketch notes

**Web Analytics:** measuring, collecting, analyzing, and reporting data collected from the Internet, most often in conjunction with website usage, for the purposes of improving performance and the user experience

# Resources
## The Tools for Your Toolbox

I love the image of tools in a toolbox as an analogy for the talents, skills, and resources we possess and put to use toward completing our daily work and building our businesses. Think of this collection of resources—books, magazines, websites, schools, and templates—as your starter set of tools.

## Read, Read, and Read Some More

The following books from highly regarded thought leaders are valuable resources on design thinking and its affiliated methodologies, such as innovation, change management, and culture. Some are highly theoretical; some are not. All will give you additional perspectives that I think you'll find valuable.

## Books

Tim Brown, *Change by Design: How Design Thinking Transforms Organizations and Inspires Innovation*. New York: HarperBusiness, 2009.

Nigel Cross, *Design Thinking: Understanding How Designers Think and Work*. New York: Bloomsbury Academic, 2011.

Steve Diller, Nathan Shedroff, and Darrell Rhea, *Making Meaning: How Successful Businesses Deliver Meaningful Customer Experiences*. San Francisco: New Riders, 2008.

Hartmut Esslinger, *A Fine Line: How Design Strategies Are Shaping the Future of Business*. New Jersey: Jossey-Bass, 2009.

Dave Gray, Sunni Brown, and James Macanufo, *Gamestorming: A Playbook for Innovators, Rulebreakers, and Changemakers*. California: O'Reilly Media, 2010.

Chip Heath and Dan Heath, *Made to Stick: Why Some Ideas Survive and Others Die*. New York: Random House, 2007.

Chip Heath and Dan Heath, *Switch: How to Change Things When Change Is Hard*. New York: Crown Business, 2010.

Tom Kelley, *The Art of Innovation: Lessons in Creativity from IDEO, America's Leading Design Firm*. New York: Crown Business, 2001.

Tom Kelley, *The Ten Faces of Innovation: IDEO's Strategies for Defeating the Devil's Advocate and Driving Creativity throughout Your Organization*. New York: Currency/Doubleday, 2005.

Roger L. Martin, *The Design of Business: Why Design Thinking Is the Next Competitive Advantage*. New York: Harvard Business School Press, 2009.

Grant David McCracken, *Culture and Consumption II: Markets, Meaning, and Brand Management (v.2)*. Indiana: Indiana University Press, 2005.

Marty Neumeier, *The Designful Company: How to Build a Culture of Nonstop Innovation*. New York: New Riders, 2008.

Dev Patnaik, *Wired to Care: How Companies Prosper When They Create Widespread Empathy*. New Jersey: FT Press, 2009.

Daniel H. Pink, *A Whole New Mind: Why Right-Brainers Will Rule the Future*. New York: Riverhead Trade, 2006

Dov Seidman, *How: Why HOW We Do Anything Means Everything*. New Jersey: Wiley, 2011.

Nathan Shedroff, *Design Is the Problem: The Future of Design Must Be Sustainable*. New York: Rosenfeld Media, 2009.

Robert I. Sutton, *Weird Ideas That Work: How to Build a Creative Company*. New York: Free Press, 2007.

# Never Stop Learning

The Internet and its vast stores of information, for all of its timewasters and nonsense, is our only constantly evolving real-time resource for the latest news, innovations, and developments in design thinking and its related disciplines. The list below includes my go-to resources.

# Websites, Blogs, and Online Tools

- *Smashing Magazine*: www.smashingmagazine.com. Although it's targeted toward web designers and developers, it contains great perspectives on user experience and design that can be applied across the board.

- *Fast Company*: www.fastcompany.com. The website of one of today's top business magazines is lush with valuable insights on trends and interviews with up-and-coming leaders. To get the full content—and to enjoy the iPad and iPhone apps—you should subscribe. Its value is far beyond its cost.

- *Inc.*: www.inc.com. Another website for a top business magazine, this one leans more toward advice, tools, and growth-specific content.

- GOOD: www.good.is. When you need a healthy dose of inspiration, a reminder about why doing good is as important as doing well, or proof that there's more to life and business than the bottom line, this is your best resource.

- Mashable: www.mashable.com. Hands down, this is the ultimate source for news related to social media and digital innovation.

- Tech Crunch: www.techcrunch.com. Synonymous with technology news, Tech Crunch also provides great content on start-ups and digital innovation.

- Design Thinking—Thoughts by Tim Brown: www.designthinking.ideo.com. If there was a god of design thinking, Tim would be it.

- *Psychology Today*: www.psychologytoday.com. I personally find the content fascinating and useful in my professional and personal lives.

- Survey Gizmo: www.surveygizmo.com. This is a great professional resource for building, distributing, and evaluating survey research. Its brand carries a stronger message than other web-based offerings.

- Survey System Sample Size Calculator: www.surveysystem.com/sscalc.htm. I use this tool when I'm trying to gauge whether a survey would be appropriate for my research project and, if so, what sample size I'll need.

- User Effect 25-point Website Usability Checklist: www.usereffect.com/topic/25-point-website-usability-checklist. This tool is a great, covers-it-all checklist for website usability. Use it when you build a new site or refresh an existing one.

- Information Architecture Institute: www.iainstitute.org. IAI is simply the go-to source for information architecture.

- American Institute of Graphic Arts (AIGA): www.aiga.org. Another go-to source but not just for graphic arts; the information frequently applies to all forms of design.

- HowTo.Gov/Customer Experience: www.howto.gov/customer-experience. Seriously, the federal government has some great information on customer experience. It's presented in terms useful for government agencies, and it's applicable in multiple business sectors.

- Eisman Center for Color Information and Training: www.colorexpert.com. It *is* possible to know the psychological and branding implications of color in great depth, and Letrice Eisman is the expert.

# Form Follows Function

To pursue a more in-depth or specialized formal study in design thinking and other related subjects, we are fortunate to have a good number of top-rated programs based in the United States. (I've included one from London, not only because it is a good program, but also because I'd like to go there some day.)

## Education Programs

California College of the Arts: www.cca.edu

Cranfield University/University of the Arts, London: www.cranfield.ac.uk

Illinois Institute of Technology: www.iit.edu

Pratt Institute: www.pratt.edu

Rhode Island School of Design: www.risd.edu

Savannah College of Art and Design: www.scad.edu

Stanford University Design School: www.dschool.standford.edu

Suffolk University: www.suffolk.edu

# Templates

I unabashedly love templates. They are adaptable and incorporate best practices. More important, they provide a starting point so you aren't staring at a blank page wondering what to put on it. I have included two templates here for documents that tend to present the biggest challenges: a moderator's guide for a focus group and a marketing template. Use them as you will.

Moderator's Guide
Example for a Quick Service Restaurant

Project Schedule

| Market | Day | Time | Segment | Number of respondents |
|--------|-----|------|---------|----------------------|
| In what city is this focus group? | What's the date? | What's the time? | Describe the group, e.g. women age 25+, HHI $60K, etc. | How many are participating in this group? |
| | | | | |
| | | | | |
| | | | | |

I.     **INTRODUCTIONS + RULES**               **[10 minutes]**
- Moderator intro
- THANK YOU for being here today and for providing us with your insight and opinions
- Rules of the room: Microphones, video/audio taping, speak one at a time in an audible voice
- Rules of the road: Here to listen to different opinions, everyone's perspective matters, no right or wrong answers, have fun, get to know others
- Respondent intro
    1. Name, where from, how long in given market, who lives at home, job/what keeps you busy these days
    2. Favorite program, types of media you watch/interact with
    3. Favorite indulgence at a quick service restaurant

II.    **OVERALL QSR HABITS + PRACTICES**       **[10 minutes]**
*Today we are going to have some fun, talking about Quick Service Restaurants and what restaurants you like to eat at. So to begin, let's set the stage....*

1. What makes a restaurant a Quick Service Restaurant? What are some examples of Quick Service Restaurants?

2. Tell me where [name of restaurant] you typically eat this type of food? Not just where you eat most often, but the range of places you eat. [MODERATOR to list on easel, starting to **draw a landscape** – i.e. where they eat most often written in larger/bolder print]

3. If you think back over the past year or so, what have been the **biggest changes** in your own personal dining habits?
    - Probe on: Changes in restaurants, changes in frequency – do you visit more/less often + why? changes in types of food, health-consciousness, looking for better prices etc.

III.   **FOCUS IN ON QSR CLIENT**               **[10 minutes]**
*OK, let's shift our focus and talk about one of these restaurants in particular – [Insert Client Name]...*

**Figure D-1a.** Sample moderator's guide (page 1). Source: Jessica Massay, JUMP Insights. Used with permission

Moderator's Guide
Example for a Quick Service Restaurant

1. What's the first thing that comes to mind when you think of *[Insert Client Name]*? [**Top-of-mind associations**]

2. What does *[Insert Client Name]* do **Differently** than other Quick Service Restaurants? Is there something they do **Better**? Is there anything they don't do as well? *(This will get us to* current *positioning/perceptions before reviewing advertising)*
   - PROBE on: Customization, Specialized Items, Service (table + overall), Quality ingredients, Different products, Open 24 hours etc.
   - PROBE: What gives you this impression of *[Insert Client Name]*? Experience, Advertising, What others say etc.
   - We will have time to deep dive into 1-2 competitors here.

3. If you had to give me **5 words** that sum up what *[Insert Client Name]* is all about **TODAY**, what would they be? [Moderator to write up on easel for later reference] Has this changed? If so, why?

IV.  **REVIEW OF** *[Insert Client Name]* **ADVERTISING**                    [35 minutes]
     *Let's switch gears a bit… now we are going to have some fun and look at some [Insert Client Name] advertising – you are my expert panel and I need your opinions on these ads…*

1. Who **has seen** any *[Insert Client Name]* advertising? If so, what do you recall about it?

2. Has it **changed** over the years? If so, how?
   - PROBE on: Tone, Feel, Message, Testimonials, Products etc.
   - Compare – 5 years ago vs. today

3. Let's take a look at a few *[Insert Client Name]* **ads**. As we watch each one, please take a minute to jot down a few things on your paper for me:
   - A rating from 1 to 5 where 1 = Doesn't connect with me at all and 5= this ad totally gets me and makes me want to go to *[Insert Client Name]* [MODERATOR to write on board for reference]
   - Any top-of-mind words that come to mind as you watch the ad – *These words don't have to be in the commercial.*
   - Have any of you seen this particular commercial before?

4. For each ad, debrief on the following:
   - **Main message** + comprehension [PROBE on **brand vs. product messaging balance**]
   - **Likes/dislikes**, anything confusing
   - **Relevance** – who is this ad for? Is it talking to you? Why/why not? Does it feel "real" – relevant to Latinos or does it feel like just a translation?
   - **Uniqueness** – how is this different than ads you see for other QSR? Is it better, worse, just different?
   - **Feeling** – how does this ad make you feel about Whataburger?
   - **Action** - Does it make you want to do anything right now?

**Figure D-1b.** Sample moderator's guide (page 2)

Moderator's Guide
Example for a Quick Service Restaurant

5. Specific probes on advertising:

- Brand – What is the role of *[Insert Client Name]* in this ad? How do you know / what tells you that message?
- Product – What does the product tell you about *[Insert Client Name]*?
- Motivation – What do you want to do after seeing this ad? Does it motivate you to do something? If so, what?

6. Is there anything missing? Is there anything that *[Insert Client Name]* **should/could show or talk** about that would be interesting and important to you as a consumer?


**V.   PRODUCT / MENU SESSION**                              **[25 minutes]**
OK, this is the last part of our group and we're going to make it a working session – an idea session – what I'm looking for from you now is ideas – any idea is a good one!

[MODERATOR to put up a **big clock** with key dayparts outlined - morning, mid-morning, lunch, afternoon, dinner, late night. Also, hand out *[Insert Client Name]* menu sheets for each respondent and put one up on PPT]

1. The first thing I'll ask you to do is tell me your favorite products to eat at *[Insert Client Name]*. Let's do this by time of day – tell me your favorite for breakfast, lunch, dinner, snack....**[Top of mind, before seeing menu]**

2. Now let's take a look at a *[Insert Client Name]* menu. Can you **circle** the items you eat most frequently? Now, can you **underline** the items that you eat sometimes? Can you put an "X" through the items you never order?

   - Tell me a little bit more about why you LOVE about the items you eat most often?
   - How about the items you eat less often – what's holding you back?
   - Finally, the items you don't eat – what's stopping you? Time permitting only

3. Look at the items you love – and tell me:
   - WHO do you usually eat this item with? Who are you with? Do they order the same thing or something different?
   - WHEN do you eat this? What time of day is it "right" for? When else would you consider eating it? When would you NOT consider ordering it?
   - Is there something on the menu that you would like to see offered at another time of day? Why? Are there any items that are only for specific times of day?

4. How about customization? How/Do you customize your order?
   - PROBE: bacon, salsa, cheese, jalapenos etc. What do you do to make it "your" order?

5. Is there something missing from the current menu that you would like to see *[Insert Client Name]* offer? If so, what would it be? What would make you go to *[Insert Client Name]* even more often?

**Figure D-1c.** Sample moderator's guide (page 3)

Moderator's Guide
Example for a Quick Service Restaurant

VI.   CLOSE                                            [5 minutes]

To finish, we are going to look at one print ad from *[Insert Client Name]*:
- What do you think about the bilingual offer?
- Which would you read?
- What are your first thoughts about the offer – appealing or not? Why?

Address any outstanding comments from the client
Thank respondents for their time and information

**Figure D-1d.** Sample moderator's guide (page 4)

**Marketing Plan Template**

**I. The Business Case**

- What is the business case for what you want to accomplish?
- One to two paragraphs
- Use supporting data

**II. Strategic Overview**

- A description of your business/product/service and why it effectively satisfies the business case. One to two paragraphs

**III. Marketing Objectives**

- Use bullet points
- Illustrate the "big picture" you want to accomplish
- No more than five objectives or this will get unwieldly

**IV. Communications Objectives**

- More detailed than the marketing objectives
- Focus on tactics

**V. Target Audiences**

- One or two audiences that will provide you with greatest opportunity for a return. Use research to guide you
- Use a narrative description of the target audience
- Use any relevant demographic data

**VI. Marketing Strategies**

- Now the plan begins to show some greater detail
- Include more specification as to how to accomplish the plan's marketing objectives
- Outline should be broad strokes of activity

**VII. Key and Supporting Messages**

- Can be omitted depending upon the process you and/or your team went through
- Includes one key message and relevant supporting messages
- Consider specific word choices

**VIII. Tactical Plan**

- Outline the nitty-gritty details of your marketing plan
- Articulate what you'll do to follow your strategies and accomplish your objectives
- Include as much detail as possible for each of the resources you listed as tactics

**Figure D-2a.** Marketing plan template (page 1)

- Create a timeline to delineate what happens and when

**IX. Measurement**

- Addresses how you will measure your efforts in all areas
- Decide if you want to measure the performance of the marketing campaign as a whole or each tactic individually
- Identify KPIs and track performance against them

**Figure D-2b.** Marketing plan template (p. 2)

# I

# Index

## A

Archaeologist, qualitative research, 21
    customer intercepts, 22–23
    focus groups, 23–25
Atmosphere light testing

## B

Brainstorming process, 97
Branding strategy, 118
Business strategy
    circles of influence, 32
    context map
        conversation drifts, 36
        Economic Climate, 36
        external environment, 35
        interactive and advance
            preparation, 35
        JDI Deep Sea Excursions, 37
        Political Factors, 36
        reinforcement, 37
        systemic view, 35
        Technology Factors, 36–37
    stakeholder vision exercise, 120
    stakeholder visioning, 37
    start-up leadership, 119
    SWOT and competitive analyses, 32

## C

Change designing
    3-12-3 activity, 124
    distinctive quality, 93
    3-12-3 exercise, 97

forest and trees activity
    forest issue, 96
    opportunity/portend disaster, 94
    in progress, 95
    ramifications, 96
    sorting tool, 94
    talent acquisition, 95
    team evaluation, 95
    themes, 95
Forest and Trees exercise, 123
gut instinct, 93
impact and effort matrix
    amount of effort, 100
    categorizing actions, 99
    evaluation and mapping, 99
    financial planning firm and talent
        acquisition, 101
    generate ideas, 100
    implementation, 100
    in progress, 99
    ready for input, 100
Customer journey
    map (CJM), 46, 70
    browsing product, 48
    check-out path, 49
    enter path, 49
    Foot and Gait Analysis, 49
    footwear fitting, 49
    greeting path, 49
    label square, 48
    outcomes, 49
    store path, 47
    store's operating hours/review
        products, 47

## D, E

Design thinking
   co-creation, 133
   collaborative, 133
   context, 134
   culture of collaboration, 134
   customer engagement, 134
   customer experience, 134
   deep design, 134
   deeper dive
      competitor benefits, 5
      definition, 7
      hospital leadership, 5
      ideation, 7
      prototype, 10
      test (see Testing)
   define phase, 3
   definition, 2
   design strategy, 134
   digital storytelling, 134
   empathy, 134
   experience design, 134
   exploratory approach, 2
   feedback loop, 134
   futurist, 134
   getting traction, 134
   human capital, 134
   ideate phase, 4
   ideation, 134
   ideograph, 135
   integrated thinking, 135
   intrapreneur, 135
   iterate, 135
   iterative and rapid process, 3
   key performance indicators (KPIs), 135
   mind map, 135
   open-ended, open-minded and
      iterative process, 2
   prototype, 4, 135
   radical innovation, 135
   research (see Research)
   roadmap, 135
   scenario planning, 135
   social entrepreneur, 135
   social innovation, 135
   stakeholders, 135
   storytelling, 135
   test, 4
   understand phase, 3
   user-centered design, 136
   user-centered research, 136
   user experience (UX), 136
   visual thinking, 136
   web analytics, 136
Digital customer experiences
   mobile experience
      budget-friendly, 63
      CSS media query, 62
      digital designers, 62
      financial resources, 63
      mobile application, 61
      organization leadership, 63
      responsive web design, 62
   online experiences
      (see Online experiences)
   social media experience
      clothing retailers, 64
      desirable response, 65
      powerful communication
         tool, 64
      reputation management, 65
      wider audience, 64

## F

Foot and Gait Analysis, 49

## G

Gamestorming, 25
Growth designing
   admirably tall tree, 104
   alive and thriving, 104
   business operations, 109
   20-20 exercise, 105
      adding team, 107
      flip-chart paper, 105
      history aids, 105
      identify patterns, 108
      nursery timeline, 106
      team input, 108
      text and images, 107
   metaphorical box, 109
   new product/service, 109
   rapid brainstorming matrix, 114
   rate variation, 104
   VP design, 110

## H, I

Human element
    CJM
        browsing product, 48
        check-out path, 49
        enter path, 49
        Foot and Gait Analysis, 49
        footwear fitting, 49
        greeting path, 49
        label square, 48
        objective, 47
        outcomes, 49
        store path, 47
        store's operating hours/review
            products, 47
    empathy map
        activity diagram, 45
        exercise, 44
        inevitable brainstorming, 46
        map creation, 44
        specialty running store, 46

## J

JDI Deep Sea Excursions, 37

## K

Key performance indicators
        (KPIs), 87, 135

## L

Live customer experiences
    Bricks-and-Mortar location, 40
    code of conduct, 50
    color theory
        cool colors, 43
        evolution, 42
        marketing role, 42
        warm colors, 42
    human element (see Human element)
    5 Whys activity, 122

## M, N

Marketing design
    brand DNA
        chart completed, 82
        DNA chart, 79
        DNA definition, 78
        emotional aspects, 81
        health care start-up, 79
        internal and external, 82
        P&G product brands, 83
        quadrants chart, 80
        rational aspects, 80
    plans
        business case, 84
        communications objectives, 85
        Doctor Is In activity, 89
        key and supporting
            messages, 86
        marketing objectives, 85
        marketing strategy, 86
        measurement, 87
        strategic overview, 84
        tactical plan, 86
        target audiences, 85
Metrics
    churn rate, 130
    content subscriptions, 129
    foot traffic, 128
    impressions, 129
    inquiry, 128
    iterative process, 131
    measuring performance, 130
    page view, 129
    rating satisfaction, 130
    referrals, 128
    sales, 128
    web-based communication
        specifically, 129

## O, P

Online experiences
    information architecture, 54
    navigability, 57
        navigation descriptive, 57
        serial position effect, 58
        top/left-side orientation, 57
    usability
        effective usability test, 60
        functional website, 59
        graphic design, 59

## Q

Qualitative research, 19
Quantitative research, 18

# R

Research
    archaeologist
        customer intercepts, 22–23
        focus groups, 23–25
    definition, 18
    devil's advocate tool
        Cannonball, 29
        5 Whys, 28–29
    equalizer, 20–21
    hybrid research tool, 125
    interpreters
        Dot Voting, 27
        photo sort exercise, 26–27
    qualitative, 19, 125
    quantitative, 18, 125

# S

Service delivery pathways
    customer journey map, 70
    efficiency and effectiveness, 70
    inquiry form, 71
    online/offline formats, 70, 72
    potential abandonment point, 74
    virtual assistant services, 72

Services
    affordable, accessible, and
        user-friendly, 68
    customer problem, 68
    intangible services, 69
    SaaS company, 68
    solve entrepreneur problem, 68
    virtual assistant service, 68–69

Software as a service (SaaS), 68

Strengths, weaknesses, opportunities,
        threats (SWOT) analyses, 32

# T, U, V, W, X, Y, Z

Testing
    atmosphere light, 13
    audio and video record, 12
    business entity, 12
    compare-and-contrast
        activity, 14
    demographics, 12
    diversity, 12
    easy and inexpensive, 11
    expectant moms, 13
    impartial moderator/facilitator, 13
    individual group analysis, 14
    location, 13
    neonatal care unit, 13
    nondisclosure/noncompete
        agreement, 12
    parameters, 15
    physicians and nurses, 13
    testing participants, 11
    themes, 14

# Get the eBook for only $10!

---

Now you can take the weightless companion with you anywhere, anytime. Your purchase of this book entitles you to 3 electronic versions for only $10.

---

This Apress title will prove so indispensible that you'll want to carry it with you everywhere, which is why we are offering the eBook in 3 formats for only $10 if you have already purchased the print book.

Convenient and fully searchable, the PDF version enables you to easily find and copy code—or perform examples by quickly toggling between instructions and   applications. The MOBI format is ideal for your Kindle, while the ePUB can be utilized on a variety of mobile devices.

Go to www.apress.com/promo/tendollars to purchase your companion eBook.

# Other Apress Business Titles You Will Find Useful

**Startup**
Ready
978-1-4302-4218-5

**Metrics**
Klubeck
978-1-4302-3726-6

**Inventors at Work**
Stern
978-1-4302-4506-3

**How to Get Government Contracts**
Smotrova-Taylor
978-1-4302-4497-4

**Health Care Reform Simplified, 2nd Edition**
Parks
978-1-4302-4896-5

**Tax Strategies for the Small Business Owner**
Fox
978-1-4302-4842-2

**Common Sense**
Tanner
978-1-4302-4152-2

**Plan to Turn Your Company Around in 90 Days**
Lack
978-1-4302-4668-8

**Improving Profit**
Cleland
978-1-4302-6307-4

## Available at www.apress.com

Printed in Great Britain
by Amazon